D0531995

BROILED PINK GRAPEFRUIT

SERVES 4

A quick, simple breakfast; it may be speedy but its flavor is sensational.

2 Florida pink grapefruit
2 tbsp honey
pinch of ground allspice
mint sprigs to garnish (optional)

≈ Cut the skin away from the grapefruit, remove any remaining pith and cut each grapefruit into quarters. Place the quarters in a heatproof shallow dish.

≈ Mix together the honey and allspice and spoon over the grapefruit pieces. Cook under the broiler for 5 minutes. Serve garnished with mint if desired.

NUTRITION FACTS		
Serving Size 1 (134g)		
Calories 69		Calories from Fat 0
		% Daily Value
Total Fat 0g		0%
Saturated Fat 0g		0%
Monounsaturated Fat 0.0g		0%
Polyunsaturated Fat 0.0g		0%
Cholesterol 0mg		0%
Sodium 1mg		0%
Total Carbohydrate 18g		6%
Dietary Fiber 1g		6%
Sugars 16g		0%
Protein 1g		0%

Percent daily values are based on a 2000 calorie diet

OATMEAL WITH POACHED FRUIT

SERVES 4

A quick oatmeal which can be made in advance or the night before. Hearty and filling, the poached fruit sets it off perfectly.

1⅔ cups oatmeal

4¼ cups skim milk

6 oz plums, halved, pitted, and sliced

8 tbsp honey

≈ Place the oatmeal in a pan with the milk. Bring to a boil, reduce the heat and simmer for 5 minutes, stirring until thickened.

≈ Meanwhile, place the plums in a saucepan with 2 tablespoons of honey and ⅔ cup water. Bring to a boil, reduce heat and simmer for 5 minutes until softened. Drain well.

≈ Spoon the porridge into individual bowls and top with the poached plums. Serve hot with the remaining 6 tablespoons of honey.

NUTRITION FACTS	
Serving Size 1 (359g)	
Calories 310	Calories from Fat 18
	% Daily Value
Total Fat 2g	2%
Saturated Fat 1g	7%
Monounsaturated Fat 0.3g	0%
Polyunsaturated Fat 0.3g	0%
Cholesterol 5mg	2%
Sodium 183mg	8%
Total Carbohydrate 66g	22%
Dietary Fiber 2g	7%
Sugars 46g	0%
Protein 11g	0%

Percent daily values are based on a 2000 calorie diet

BREAKFAST HASH

MAKES 4

For a speedier breakfast, cook the potatoes for this tasty dish the evening before and store in a sealed bag in the refrigerator until required.

3 cups peeled, cubed potatoes

1 tbsp sunflower oil

1 red bell pepper, seeded, and halved

1 green bell pepper, seeded, and halved

2 tomatoes, diced

1½ cups open cap mushrooms, peeled, quartered

2 tbsp fresh chopped parsley

ground black pepper

≈ Cook the potatoes in boiling water for 7 minutes, drain well. Heat the sunflower oil in a large skillet, add the potatoes and cook for 10 minutes, stirring.

≈ Chop the red and green bell peppers and add to the skillet with the tomatoes and mushrooms. Cook for 5 minutes, stirring constantly, add the chopped parsley, season to taste and serve.

NUTRITION FACTS	
Serving Size 1 (277g)	
Calories 179	Calories from Fat 36
	% Daily Value
Total Fat 4g	6%
Saturated Fat 0g	2%
Monounsaturated Fat 1.6g	0%
Polyunsaturated Fat 1.6g	0%
Cholesterol 0mg	0%
Sodium 88mg	4%
Total Carbohydrate 34g	11%
Dietary Fiber 4g	15%
Sugars 6g	0%
Protein 4g	0%

Percent daily values are based on a 2000 calorie diet

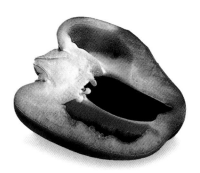

Breakfast Hash ▶

FRUIT KABOBS

SERVES 4

The perfect way to present fresh fruit, these lightly broiled kabobs with a hint of mint make a refreshing start to the day.

2 tbsp fine granulated sugar

2 mint sprigs, plus extra for garnish

1 papaya, halved, seeded, and chopped into 2-inch squares

1 mango, pitted and chopped into 2-inch squares

1 star fruit, sliced

2 Chinese gooseberries, thickly sliced

≈ Soak four wooden skewers in water for 30 minutes. Remove when ready to use. Place the sugar, mint, and ⅔ cup water in a pan. Heat gently to dissolve the sugar and then bring to a boil until reduced by half. Discard the mint.

≈ Thread the fruit onto the skewers, alternating the varieties. Brush with the syrup and broil for 10 minutes, turning and brushing until heated through. Serve hot, garnished with mint.

HASH BROWN POTATOES WITH BAKED BEANS

SERVES 6

These golden potato cakes are served with a spicy bean dish, and are perfect for mopping up the delicious juices. Make the bean dish in advance and keep in the refrigerator until morning. Simply heat the beans in a pan over a gentle heat.

≈ Drain the soaked beans and rinse well under cold water. Drain and put in a large saucepan with 2 cups of water. Bring the beans to a boil and boil rapidly for 10 minutes. Reduce the heat to a simmer, cover and cook for 1 hour or until the beans are cooked, topping up the water if necessary. Drain the beans and return them to the pan. Stir in the vegetable broth, dried mustard, onion, molasses, tomatoes, tomato paste, and basil. Season well and cook for 15 minutes or until the vegetables have cooked.

≈ Meanwhile, make the potato cakes while the beans are cooking. Cook the potatoes in boiling water for 20 minutes or until soft. Drain well and mash with the milk.

≈ Add the onion and garlic, mixing well and form into twelve equal-sized cakes. Brush a non-stick skillet with the oil and warm over a medium heat. Cook the potato cakes for 15–20 minutes, turning once until golden brown. Serve hot with the baked beans.

NUTRITION FACTS	
Serving Size 1 (260g)	
Calories 154	Calories from Fat 9
	% Daily Value
Total Fat 1g	1%
Saturated Fat 0g	0%
Monounsaturated Fat 0.0g	0%
Polyunsaturated Fat 0.2g	0%
Cholesterol 0mg	0%
Sodium 12mg	0%
Total Carbohydrate 37g	12%
Dietary Fiber 6g	23%
Sugars 25g	0%
Protein 1g	0%

Percent daily values are based on a 2000 calorie diet

Hash Brown Potatoes with Baked Beans

For the baked beans

1¼ cups dried navy beans, soaked
    overnight
⅔ cup vegetable broth
½ tsp dried mustard
1 onion, chopped
2 tbsp dark molasses
1 cup tomatoes, peeled, chopped
1 tbsp tomato paste
1 tbsp fresh chopped basil
ground black pepper

For the potato cakes

3 cups peeled, cubed potatoes
2 tbsp skim milk
1 onion, chopped
1 garlic clove, minced
2 tsp sunflower oil

NUTRITION FACTS	
Serving Size 1 (194g)	
Calories 241	Calories from Fat 18

	% Daily Value
Total Fat 2g	4%
Saturated Fat 0g	2%
Monounsaturated Fat 0.7g	0%
Polyunsaturated Fat 0.9g	0%
Cholesterol 0mg	0%
Sodium 125mg	5%
Total Carbohydrate 46g	15%
Dietary Fiber 8g	30%
Sugars 3g	0%
Protein 11g	0%

Percent daily values are based on a 2000 calorie diet

BREAD PUDDING

SERVES 8

Renowned as a delicious, but fattening dish, this savory bread pudding is the perfect example of adapting a recipe to low-fat without compromising on taste.

6 slices whole wheat bread, with crusts removed

1 tbsp polyunsaturated margarine

1 red bell pepper, halved and seeded

1 green bell pepper, halved and seeded

2 tomatoes, chopped

½ cup low-fat Cheddar cheese, shredded

2 egg whites, beaten

2 cups skim milk

ground black pepper

≈ Spread the bread with the margarine and cut each slice into four triangles by cutting on the diagonal.

≈ Place the peppers skin side uppermost on a rack and broil for 10 minutes until blackened. Place in a polythene bag with tongs, seal and let cool. Peel off the the skins and discard. Slice the peppers into thin strips.

≈ Layer the bread, peppers, tomatoes, and half of the cheese in a large shallow ovenproof dish. Mix the egg white and milk together and pour over the bread. Allow to sit for 30 minutes.

≈ Sprinkle the remaining cheese over the dish and season. Cook in the oven at 325°F for 45 minutes until set and risen. Serve hot.

NUTRITION FACTS	
Serving Size 1 (165g)	
Calories 112	Calories from Fat 18

	% Daily Value
Total Fat 2g	4%
Saturated Fat 1g	3%
Monounsaturated Fat 1.0g	0%
Polyunsaturated Fat 0.7g	0%
Cholesterol 1mg	0%
Sodium 214mg	9%
Total Carbohydrate 16g	5%
Dietary Fiber 2g	9%
Sugars 5g	0%
Protein 8g	0%

Percent daily values are based on a 2000 calorie diet

BREAKFAST MUFFINS

MAKES 12

Breakfast wouldn't be breakfast without muffins. This healthy version gives you all the goodness you'd want from an old favorite.

¾ cup whole wheat flour

1 cup all-purpose flour

1 tbsp baking powder

⅔ cup natural muesli

2 tbsp chopped dates

2 tsp granulated brown sugar

1 egg white, whisked

⅔ cup skim milk

2 tbsp polyunsaturated margarine, melted

≈ Place the flours, baking powder, muesli, dates, and brown sugar in a bowl. In a separate bowl, mix together the egg white, milk, and margarine. Pour into the dry ingredients in one go. Stir gently.

≈ Spoon the mixture into eight muffin cases to two-thirds full. Bake in the oven at 425°F for 20–25 minutes until risen and golden. Serve warm.

NUTRITION FACTS	
Serving Size 1 (46g)	
Calories 119	Calories from Fat 27

	% Daily Value
Total Fat 3g	4%
Saturated Fat 1g	3%
Monounsaturated Fat 0.9g	0%
Polyunsaturated Fat 0.7g	0%
Cholesterol 0mg	0%
Sodium 170mg	7%
Total Carbohydrate 21g	7%
Dietary Fiber 1g	5%
Sugars 5g	0%
Protein 3g	0%

Percent daily values are based on a 2000 calorie diet

Bread Pudding ▶

½ lb strawberries, hulled and
  chopped

⅔ cup cranberry juice

2 tbsp honey

½ tsp ground ginger

2 cups sparkling mineral water

ice and mint sprigs to serve

4 whole strawberries, for garnish

NUTRITION FACTS

Serving Size 1 (265g)

Calories 85	Calories from Fat 0
	% Daily Value
Total Fat 0g	0%
Saturated Fat 0g	0%
Monounsaturated Fat 0.0g	0%
Polyunsaturated Fat 0.2g	0%
Cholesterol 0mg	0%
Sodium 3mg	0%
Total Carbohydrate 21g	7%
Dietary Fiber 2g	9%
Sugars 20g	0%
Protein 1g	0%

Percent daily values are based on a 2000 calorie diet

For the biscuits

½ cup whole wheat flour

1 tsp baking powder

1 tsp superfine sugar

1 medium egg, beaten

⅓ cup skim milk

1 green dessert apple, cored and
  chopped

1 tbsp raisins

For the yogurt sauce

⅔ cup low-fat plain yogurt

½ tsp ground cinnamon

1 tsp honey

NUTRITION FACTS

Serving Size 1 (122g)

Calories 131	Calories from Fat 18
	% Daily Value
Total Fat 2g	3%
Saturated Fat 1g	4%
Monounsaturated Fat 0.7g	0%
Polyunsaturated Fat 0.3g	0%
Cholesterol 55mg	18%
Sodium 368mg	15%
Total Carbohydrate 23g	8%
Dietary Fiber 3g	10%
Sugars 11g	0%
Protein 6g	0%

Percent daily values are based on a 2000 calorie diet

STRAWBERRY COCKTAIL

SERVES 4

A refreshing breakfast cocktail with a sparkle. It is as quick and easy to make as it is to drink.

≈ Place the strawberries, cranberry juice, honey, and ginger in a food processor and blend for 30 seconds until smooth.

≈ Add the sparkling mineral water, ice, and mint. Pour into glasses, garnish, and serve immediately.

APPLE DROP BISCUITS

SERVES 4

This healthy version of a breakfast favorite is filled with chunks of crisp apple which are complemented by the cinnamon spiced yogurt sauce.

≈ Sift the flour and baking powder for the biscuits into a mixing bowl and stir in the sugar. Make a well in the center and beat in the egg and milk to make a smooth batter. Stir in the apple and raisins, mixing well.

≈ Brush a heavy based non-stick skillet with a little oil and warm over a medium heat. Divide the batter into eight equal portions and drop four portions into the skillet, spacing them well apart. Cook for 2–3 minutes until the top of each drop biscuit begins to bubble. Turn the biscuits over and cook for 1 minute. Transfer to a warmed plate and keep hot while cooking the remaining four biscuits.

≈ Mix the yogurt sauce ingredients together in a bowl and serve with the hot drop biscuits.

Apple Drop Biscuits ▶

SPICED PEARS

SERVES 4

The aroma from this dish is almost as good as the taste, and all part of the enjoyment. If liked, serve with a spoonful of plain yogurt or cottage cheese.

≈ Place the pear halves in a pan with the fruit juice, spices, raisins, and sugar. Heat gently to dissolve the sugar and then bring to a boil.

≈ Reduce the heat to a simmer and cook for a further 10 minutes until the pears are softened. Serve hot with the syrup.

4 large ripe pears, peeled, halved, and cored

1¼ cups mango juice

1 cinnamon stick, crushed

½ tsp grated nutmeg

3 tbsp raisins

2 tbsp granulated brown sugar

NUTRITION FACTS	
Serving Size 1 (259g)	
Calories 204	Calories from Fat 18
	% Daily Value
Total Fat 2g	3%
Saturated Fat 0g	0%
Monounsaturated Fat 0.1g	0%
Polyunsaturated Fat 0.2g	0%
Cholesterol 0mg	0%
Sodium 21mg	1%
Total Carbohydrate 50g	17%
Dietary Fiber 7g	27%
Sugars 37g	0%
Protein 1g	0%

Percent daily values are based on a 2000 calorie diet

SPICY FRUIT SALAD

SERVES 4

Dried fruits are filled with goodness and have a delicious, concentrated flavor of their own. With many varieties now available it is easy to mix delicious combinations to create your personal favorite fruit salad.

≈ Place the fruits in a bowl and add the cinnamon and orange juice. Cover and let soak overnight.

≈ Place the contents of the bowl in a saucepan with the mint and bring to a boil, reduce the heat to a simmer and cook for 20 minutes until the fruits have softened. Cool and transfer to the refrigerator. Cover until required.

≈ Remove the mint from the salad. Mix together the yogurt and orange rind. Serve with the fruit salad.

½ cup dried apricots

½ cup dried peaches

½ cup dried mango

½ cup dried pears

½ cup dried pitted prunes

1 tsp ground cinnamon

3¾ cups orange juice

3 mint sprigs

⅔ cup low-fat plain yogurt

grated rind of 1 orange

NUTRITION FACTS	
Serving Size 1 (370g)	
Calories 368	Calories from Fat 18
	% Daily Value
Total Fat 2g	3%
Saturated Fat 0g	2%
Monounsaturated Fat 0.5g	0%
Polyunsaturated Fat 0.3g	0%
Cholesterol 2mg	1%
Sodium 36mg	2%
Total Carbohydrate 89g	30%
Dietary Fiber 8g	31%
Sugars 70g	0%
Protein 6g	0%

Percent daily values are based on a 2000 calorie diet

Spiced Pears ▶

SIMPLE APPETIZERS AND HOT SOUPS

CRUDITÉS
WITH CHILE TOMATO DIP

SERVES 4

One of the simplest yet most popular appetizers, an array of colorful, crisp vegetables served with a delicious dip is hard to resist.

2 celery stalks, trimmed and cut into
    eight sticks
1 green bell pepper, halved, seeded,
    and cut into strips
1 carrot, cut into julienne sticks
3 cherry tomatoes
¼ cup snow peas

For the dip
1¼ cups low-fat plain yogurt
1 tbsp tomato paste
4 tbsp low-fat mayonnaise
1 green chile, chopped
1 tbsp fresh chopped parsley

≈ Prepare all the vegetables. Mix together the dip ingredients and place in a serving bowl.

≈ Place the bowl on a serving platter and arrange the vegetables around the dip. Serve immediately.

BAKED POTATO SKINS

SERVES 4

Always a firm favorite, remember to prepare the skins a day in advance for ease and speed. Pop them into the oven to warm them through before serving.

≈ Scrub the potatoes and place on a baking sheet. Cook in the oven at 400°F for 1 hour or until soft. Remove and cool. Cut the potatoes in half lengthwise and scoop out the centers with a teaspoon, leaving a ½-inch thickness shell. Sprinkle the skins with salt and place the potatoes in the oven for 10 minutes or until crisp.

≈ Mix the yogurt dip ingredients together. Mix together the mustard sauce ingredients. Finally mix the tomato salsa ingredients together. Place each dip in a separate bowl and cover until required. Serve with hot potato wedges.

NUTRITION FACTS	
Serving Size 1 (205g)	
Calories 105	Calories from Fat 18
	% Daily Value
Total Fat 2g	4%
Saturated Fat 1g	4%
Monounsaturated Fat 0.3g	0%
Polyunsaturated Fat 0.6g	0%
Cholesterol 4mg	1%
Sodium 330mg	14%
Total Carbohydrate 17g	6%
Dietary Fiber 3g	10%
Sugars 10g	0%
Protein 5g	0%

Percent daily values are based on a 2000 calorie diet

Baked Potato Skins

4 medium baking potatoes

For the yogurt dip

⅔ cup low-fat plain yogurt

2 garlic cloves, minced

1 tbsp scallions, sliced

For the mustard sauce

⅔ cup low-fat plain yogurt

2 tsp whole grain mustard

1 jalapeño chile, chopped

For the tomato salsa

2 medium tomatoes, chopped

3 tbsp red onion, chopped fine

1 tbsp fresh chopped parsley

1 green bell pepper, seeded and
    chopped

dash of sugar

NUTRITION FACTS	
Serving Size 1 (414g)	
Calories 325	Calories from Fat 18
	% Daily Value
Total Fat 2g	3%
Saturated Fat 1g	4%
Monounsaturated Fat 0.5g	0%
Polyunsaturated Fat 0.3g	0%
Cholesterol 4mg	1%
Sodium 107mg	4%
Total Carbohydrate 70g	23%
Dietary Fiber 7g	28%
Sugars 16g	0%
Protein 10g	0%

Percent daily values are based on a 2000 calorie diet

2 flour tortillas

For the filling

4 oz spinach, stems removed

4 scallions, sliced

¼ cup low-fat vegetarian cheddar
   cheese, shredded

a pinch of ground coriander

1 small celery stalk, trimmed and
   sliced

⅓ cup drained, canned corn

1 carrot, peeled and shredded

For the sauce

⅔ cup skim milk

2 tbsp cornstarch

⅔ cup vegetable broth

4 pickled jalapeño chiles, sliced

½ cup low-fat vegetarian cheese,
   shredded

1 tbsp tomato paste

1 tbsp fresh chopped basil

basil or cilantro sprigs to garnish

NUTRITION FACTS	
Serving Size 1 (221g)	
Calories 183	Calories from Fat 36
	% Daily Value
Total Fat 4g	6%
Saturated Fat 1g	6%
Monounsaturated Fat 1.0g	0%
Polyunsaturated Fat 0.7g	0%
Cholesterol 8mg	3%
Sodium 652mg	27%
Total Carbohydrate 25g	8%
Dietary Fiber 3g	12%
Sugars 5g	0%
Protein 13g	0%

Percent daily values are based on a 2000 calorie diet

Vegetable Enchiladas

VEGETABLE KABOBS

SERVES 6

Perfect for vegetable lovers. This colorful combination of vegetables, marinated in vermouth, is served on a bed of bulghar wheat lightly flavored with cilantro.

≈ Prepare all the vegetables and place in a shallow dish. Mix together the vermouth, oil, 2 tablespoons of the lemon juice, garlic, half of the cilantro and half of the lemon rind. Pour over the vegetables, cover and marinate for 2 hours.

≈ Meanwhile, place the bulghar wheat in a bowl, pour over 1¼ cups boiling water. Let sit for 30 minutes or until the water is absorbed. Drain if necessary and stir in the remaining lemon juice and cilantro. Season.

≈ Remove the vegetables from the marinade and thread onto four skewers. Broil for 10 minutes, turning until cooked through. Serve the bulghar wheat with the kabobs.

1 zucchini, sliced

1 yellow bell pepper, seeded and cubed

4 baby corn, halved

4 button mushrooms

1 small red bell pepper, seeded and cubed

½ cup vermouth

1 tbsp olive oil

4 tbsp lemon juice

1 garlic clove, minced

2 tbsp fresh chopped cilantro

grated rind of 1 lemon

⅔ cup bulghar wheat

ground black pepper.

VEGETABLE ENCHILADAS

SERVES 4

This is a vegetarian version of the Mexican dish. Here, flour tortillas are filled with a mixture of crunchy vegetables, rolled and baked with a spicy tomato sauce. Pickled jalapeño chiles have been used as they are milder in flavor than fresh chiles.

≈ Blanch the spinach for the filling in boiling water for 2–3 minutes. Drain well and put in a mixing bowl with the scallions, cheese, coriander, celery, corn, and carrot.

≈ Spoon half of the filling along one edge of each of the tortillas. Roll up the tortillas and cut in half. Put in a shallow ovenproof baking dish, seam side down.

≈ For the sauce, blend 4 tablespoons of the skim milk to a paste with the cornstarch. Heat the remaining milk and vegetable broth in a saucepan and stir in the cornstarch paste, jalapeño chiles, half of the cheese, and the tomato paste.

≈ Bring the sauce to a boil, stirring until thickened. Cook for 1 minute and pour over the tortillas in the dish. Sprinkle the remaining cheese on top and cook in the oven at 350°F for 30 minutes or until the sauce is bubbling and the cheese has melted. Garnish with cilantro or basil and serve with a small salad.

NUTRITION FACTS	
Serving Size 1 (209g)	
Calories 209	Calories from Fat 27
	% Daily Value
Total Fat 3g	5%
Saturated Fat 0g	2%
Monounsaturated Fat 1.7g	0%
Polyunsaturated Fat 0.3g	0%
Cholesterol 0mg	0%
Sodium 50mg	2%
Total Carbohydrate 35g	12%
Dietary Fiber 5g	19%
Sugars 2g	0%
Protein 4g	0%

Percent daily values are based on a 2000 calorie diet

VEGETABLE AND BEAN SOUP

SERVES 8

This is a really hearty soup, filled with goodness. It may be made with any selection of vegetables you have to hand and is perfect for making ahead and freezing.

7½ cups vegetable broth

1 onion, sliced

1 cup potato, cubed

2 carrots, peeled and sliced

1 parsnip, peeled, cored, and chopped

1 leek, sliced

¾ cup baby corn, sliced

2 garlic cloves, minced

1 tsp curry powder

1 tsp chili powder

16 oz can red kidney beans, drained

16 oz can borlotti or pinto beans, drained

ground black pepper

2 tbsp fresh chopped parsley

≈ Heat ⅔ cup of the broth in a large saucepan and cook the onion, potato, carrots, parsnip, leek, corn, and garlic for 5 minutes.

≈ Add the curry and chili powders with the remaining broth and bring the soup to a boil. Reduce the heat and simmer for 20 minutes or until the vegetables are tender. Add the drained beans and cook for a further 10 minutes. Season to taste and garnish with parsley before serving with crusty bread.

VEGETABLE JAMBALAYA

SERVES 4

This is a classic Caribbean dish, usually made with spicy sausage, but this vegetarian version packs just as much of a punch and tastes wonderful.

NUTRITION FACTS	
Serving Size 1 (348g)	
Calories 275	Calories from Fat 18
	% Daily Value
Total Fat 2g	3%
Saturated Fat 0g	1%
Monounsaturated Fat 0.0g	0%
Polyunsaturated Fat 0.4g	0%
Cholesterol 0mg	0%
Sodium 980mg	41%
Total Carbohydrate 51g	17%
Dietary Fiber 11g	43%
Sugars 4g	0%
Protein 17g	0%

Percent daily values are based on a 2000 calorie diet

≈ Cook the rices in boiling water for 20 minutes or until cooked. Drain well.

≈ Meanwhile, place the eggplant pieces in a colander, sprinkle with the salt and leave to stand for 20 minutes. Wash and pat dry with paper towels.

≈ Put the eggplant, onion, celery, and broth in a nonstick pan and cook for 5 minutes, stirring. Add the garlic, corn, beans, carrots, tomatoes, tomato paste, creole seasoning and chili sauce. Bring the mixture to a boil, reduce the heat and cook for a further 20 minutes until the vegetables are just cooked. Stir in the drained rice and cook for a further 5 minutes. Garnish with parsley and serve.

generous ¼ cup long grain white rice

¼ cup wild rice

1 eggplant, sliced and quartered

1 tsp salt

1 onion, chopped

1 celery stalk, trimmed and sliced

¾ cup vegetable broth

2 garlic cloves, minced

¾ cup baby corn

¾ cup green beans, trimmed

¾ cup baby carrots

1 cup canned chopped tomatoes

4 tsp tomato paste

1 tsp creole seasoning

1 tsp chili sauce

fresh chopped parsley to garnish

Vegetable Jambalaya

NUTRITION FACTS	
Serving Size 1 (228g)	
Calories 141	Calories from Fat 9
	% Daily Value
Total Fat 1g	2%
Saturated Fat 0g	1%
Monounsaturated Fat 0.1g	0%
Polyunsaturated Fat 0.5g	0%
Cholesterol 0mg	0%
Sodium 904mg	38%
Total Carbohydrate 29g	10%
Dietary Fiber 3g	11%
Sugars 3g	0%
Protein 6g	0%

Percent daily values are based on a 2000 calorie diet

ZUCCHINI AND MINT SOUP

SERVES 4

This delicate soup may be served both hot or cold. If serving hot, stir in the yogurt once the soup has been blended, garnish and serve immediately with hot bread or croutons.

≈ Put half of the vegetable broth in a large saucepan, add the onion and garlic and cook for 5 minutes over a gentle heat until the onion softens. Add the shredded zucchini, potato and the remaining broth. Stir in the mint and cook over a gentle heat for 20 minutes or until the potato is cooked.

≈ Transfer the soup to a food processor and blend for 10 seconds, until almost smooth. Turn the soup into a bowl, season and stir in the yogurt. Cover and chill for 2 hours. Spoon the soup into individual serving bowls or a soup tureen, garnish, and serve.

3½ cups vegetable broth

1 onion, chopped

1 garlic clove, minced

3 zucchini, shredded

1 large potato, scrubbed and
    chopped

1 tbsp fresh chopped mint

ground black pepper

⅔ cup low-fat plain yogurt

mint sprigs and zucchini strips
    to garnish

NUTRITION FACTS	
Serving Size 1 (271g)	
Calories 78	Calories from Fat 9
	% Daily Value
Total Fat 1g	2%
Saturated Fat 0g	2%
Monounsaturated Fat 0.2g	0%
Polyunsaturated Fat 0.0g	0%
Cholesterol 2mg	1%
Sodium 821mg	34%
Total Carbohydrate 14g	5%
Dietary Fiber 1g	3%
Sugars 5g	0%
Protein 4g	0%

Percent daily values are based on a 2000 calorie diet

ENDIVE AND ORANGE SALAD

SERVES 4

This recipe clears the palate for future courses. The crisp endive is complemented by the fruit and tangy dressing.

≈ Peel the oranges and remove any pith. Separate the oranges into segments, reserving segments and any juice. Cut the endives in half lengthwise. Halve and slice the pear, removing the core.

≈ Mix together the mint, honey, and vinegar. Add the orange juice and brush a little over the surface of the endives. Cook under the broiler for 2 minutes.

≈ Arrange the oranges and pear slices on a serving plate. Sprinkle with the chopped walnuts. Place the broiled endives on serving plates and spoon on the remaining dressing. Sprinkle on orange rind and serve.

2 oranges

2 heads endive

1 pear

2 tsp fresh chopped mint

1 tbsp clear honey

½ tbsp cider vinegar

2 tbsp orange juice

2 tbsp walnuts, chopped

grated rind of 1 orange

NUTRITION FACTS	
Serving Size 1 (179g)	
Calories 109	Calories from Fat 27
	% Daily Value
Total Fat 3g	4%
Saturated Fat 0g	1%
Monounsaturated Fat 0.6g	0%
Polyunsaturated Fat 1.6g	0%
Cholesterol 0mg	0%
Sodium 12mg	0%
Total Carbohydrate 22g	7%
Dietary Fiber 4g	17%
Sugars 16g	0%
Protein 2g	0%

Percent daily values are based on a 2000 calorie diet

Zucchini and Mint Soup ▶

SPINACH PÂTÉ

SERVES 8

This is a baked pâté which needs to be made well in advance of serving as it requires chilling after cooking. Be sure when draining the spinach to press out as much water as possible otherwise the mixture will be too wet. This recipe would be suitable for a lunch for four if sliced and served with salad or a tomato sauce.

¼ cup bulghar wheat

1½ lb spinach, stems removed

3 tbsp vegetable broth

1 onion, chopped

2 garlic cloves, minced

1 tbsp fresh chopped oregano

1 tbsp fresh chopped thyme

2 tsp cider vinegar

1 egg, beaten

2 tbsp fresh chopped cilantro

½ cup low-fat cheese, shredded

6–8 large lettuce leaves

NUTRITION FACTS	
Serving Size 1 (138g)	
Calories 66	Calories from Fat 18
	% Daily Value
Total Fat 2g	2%
Saturated Fat 0g	2%
Monounsaturated Fat 0.4g	0%
Polyunsaturated Fat 0.2g	0%
Cholesterol 29mg	10%
Sodium 120mg	5%
Total Carbohydrate 8g	3%
Dietary Fiber 3g	13%
Sugars 1g	0%
Protein 6g	0%

Percent daily values are based on a 2000 calorie diet

≈ Cook the bulghar wheat in boiling water for 15 minutes or until swollen and cooked. Drain well. Wash the spinach and cook in a saucepan until it begins to wilt. Drain very well and chop finely.

≈ Heat the broth in a saucepan and cook the onion and garlic for 2–3 minutes until beginning to soften. Add the bulghar wheat, oregano, thyme, and vinegar and cook for 5 minutes. Remove the saucepan from the heat and stir in the egg, chopped cilantro, cheese, and spinach.

≈ Line a 2 lb loaf pan with the lettuce leaves, allowing them to overhang the edge. Spoon the spinach mixture into the pan and fold the lettuce leaves over the top to cover the mixture completely.

≈ Cover the pan and cook the pâté in the oven at 350°F for 45–60 minutes or until firm. Allow to cool before transferring to the refrigerator to chill for 2 hours. Unmold the pâté, slice and serve with hot toast and a small salad.

MEDITERRANEAN TOASTS

SERVES 4

These bite-sized hot open sandwiches are delicious as a snack or appetizer. Use a small crusty bread such as Italian ciabatta or a French stick if preferred, using eight slices in place of four. Be sure to cook these just before serving for full flavor.

4 large, thick slices of crusty bread

2 garlic cloves, crushed

1 tbsp low-fat polyunsaturated
    spread, melted

4 ripe tomatoes, peeled and chopped

1 tbsp tomato paste

4 pitted black olives, chopped

ground black pepper

basil sprigs to garnish

NUTRITION FACTS	
Serving Size 1 (162g)	
Calories 123	Calories from Fat 27
	% Daily Value
Total Fat 3g	5%
Saturated Fat 0g	2%
Monounsaturated Fat 0.0g	0%
Polyunsaturated Fat 0.0g	0%
Cholesterol 0mg	0%
Sodium 265mg	11%
Total Carbohydrate 20g	7%
Dietary Fiber 2g	9%
Sugars 4g	0%
Protein 4g	0%

Percent daily values are based on a 2000 calorie diet

≈ Toast the slices of bread under the broiler for 2 minutes each side. Mix the garlic and low-fat spread together and drizzle onto one side of the toasted bread.

≈ Mix the tomatoes, tomato paste, and olives together, season, and spoon onto the toast. Cook under the broiler for 2–3 minutes or until hot. Remove the toasts from under the broiler and cut in half. Garnish with basil and serve.

Mediterranean Toasts ▶

MIXED BEAN
AND VEGETABLE SALAD

SERVES 4

Canned kidney beans and black-eyed beans are used in this colorful salad, but any beans you have to hand would be suitable. If you prefer to use dried beans, buy a mixed bag and soak 1¼ cups overnight before cooking and draining thoroughly.

4 oz lettuce

1¼ cups canned red kidney beans, drained

1¼ cups canned black-eyed beans, drained

1 red onion, halved and sliced

1 green bell pepper, seeded and cut into strips

1 orange bell pepper, seeded and cut into strips

¾ cup baby corn

⅔ cup broccoli florets

For the dressing

2 tbsp clear honey

2 tbsp garlic wine vinegar

2 tsp Dijon mustard

2 tsp fresh chopped parsley

ground black pepper

≈ Line a salad bowl with the lettuce.

≈ Mix the beans, onion, bell peppers, corn, and broccoli in a bowl and spoon into the lettuce lined bowl.

≈ Mix the dressing ingredients together in a screwtop jar, shake vigorously and pour over the salad. Toss well and serve with warm crusty bread.

CORN CHOWDER

SERVES 4

A classic chowder never loses its appeal. I challenge any of your guests to spot the difference in flavor from the traditional creamy recipe. Prepare in advance and freeze in convenient portion sizes for ease.

≈ Place the corn, broth, onion, and bell pepper in a pan. Blend 4 tablespoons of the milk with the cornstarch to form a paste.

≈ Bring the pan contents to a boil, reduce the heat and simmer for 20 minutes. Add the milk and cornstarch paste and bring to a boil, stirring until thickened. Stir in the cheese and chives and season. Heat until the cheese has melted, garnish, and serve.

NUTRITION FACTS	
Serving Size 1 (306g)	
Calories 482	Calories from Fat 18
	% Daily Value
Total Fat 2g	3%
Saturated Fat 0g	2%
Monounsaturated Fat 0.3g	0%
Polyunsaturated Fat 0.8g	0%
Cholesterol 0mg	0%
Sodium 38mg	2%
Total Carbohydrate 92g	31%
Dietary Fiber 20g	78%
Sugars 11g	0%
Protein 28g	0%

Percent daily values are based on a 2000 calorie diet

10 oz drained, canned corn kernels

2½ cups vegetable broth

1 red onion, diced

1 green bell pepper, seeded and
    diced

2½ cups skim milk

2 tbsp cornstarch

¾ cup low-fat Cheddar or Edam
    cheese, shredded

1 tbsp fresh snipped chives

ground black pepper

snipped chives, for garnish

Corn Chowder

NUTRITION FACTS	
Serving Size 1 (447g)	
Calories 216	Calories from Fat 36

	% Daily Value
Total Fat 4g	6%
Saturated Fat 1g	7%
Monounsaturated Fat 1.1g	0%
Polyunsaturated Fat 0.6g	0%
Cholesterol 10mg	3%
Sodium 854mg	36%
Total Carbohydrate 29g	10%
Dietary Fiber 2g	9%
Sugars 10g	0%
Protein 18g	0%

Percent daily values are based on a 2000 calorie diet

MARINATED MUSHROOMS

SERVES 4

These mushrooms are quite spicy and are delicious served with oat crackers to mop up the delicious sauce.

2½ cups button mushrooms

½ cup dry sherry

¼ cup garlic wine vinegar

¼ cup vegetable broth

2 garlic cloves, minced

1 onion, cut into eight

1 tsp mustard

1 tbsp soy sauce

2 tbsp tomato paste

1 bay leaf

≈ Place the mushrooms in a pan with the sherry, vinegar, broth, garlic, onion, mustard, soy sauce, tomato paste, and bay leaf. Heat gently for 10 minutes. Allow to cool, remove bay leaf and transfer to a serving dish. Cover and chill until required. Serve with oat cakes and salad.

NUTRITION FACTS	
Serving Size 1 (103g)	
Calories 44	Calories from Fat 9
	% Daily Value
Total Fat 1g	1%
Saturated Fat 0g	0%
Monounsaturated Fat 0.2g	0%
Polyunsaturated Fat 0.1g	0%
Cholesterol 0mg	0%
Sodium 368mg	15%
Total Carbohydrate 7g	2%
Dietary Fiber 1g	5%
Sugars 2g	0%
Protein 2g	0%

Percent daily values are based on a 2000 calorie diet

ASPARAGUS WITH BELL PEPPER SAUCE

SERVES 4

This bright red bell pepper sauce looks terrific spooned over asparagus spears. If you don't want to make a spicy sauce, either reduce the amount of chili sauce added, or omit it altogether.

For the sauce

3 red bell peppers, halved
   and seeded

2 cups vegetable broth

1 tsp chili sauce

juice of 1 lemon

1 garlic clove, minced

1 lb asparagus spears, trimmed

grated rind of 1 lemon

parsley sprigs to garnish

≈ To make the sauce, cook the bell peppers under a hot broiler, skin side uppermost for 5 minutes until the skin begins to blacken and blister. Transfer the peppers to a plastic bag using tongs, seal and leave for 20 minutes. Peel the skin from the bell peppers and discard.

≈ Roughly chop the bell peppers and put them in a saucepan with the broth, chili sauce, lemon juice, and garlic.

≈ Cook over a gentle heat for 20 minutes or until the peppers are tender. Transfer the sauce to a food processor and blend for 10 seconds. Return the purée to the saucepan and heat through gently.

≈ Meanwhile, tie the asparagus spears into four equal bundles. Stand upright in a steamer or saucepan filled with boiling water and cook for 10–15 minutes until tender. Remove the asparagus from the pan and untie the bundles. Arrange on four serving plates and spoon the sauce over the top. Sprinkle the lemon rind on top, garnish with parsley and serve.

Asparagus with Bell Pepper Sauce ▶

NUTRITION FACTS	
Serving Size 1 (303g)	
Calories 57	Calories from Fat 9
	% Daily Value
Total Fat 1g	2%
Saturated Fat 0g	1%
Monounsaturated Fat 0.0g	0%
Polyunsaturated Fat 0.4g	0%
Cholesterol 0mg	0%
Sodium 937mg	39%
Total Carbohydrate 10g	3%
Dietary Fiber 3g	12%
Sugars 6g	0%
Protein 4g	0%

Percent daily values are based on a 2000 calorie diet

MEDITERRANEAN SALAD

SERVES 4

A ny combination of vegetables would be delicious steeped in this tomato and garlic sauce. Be sure to chill the dish well before serving and have crusty bread to hand to mop up the juices.

1¼ cups vegetable broth

1 onion, chopped fine

1 garlic clove, minced

¼ cup dry white wine

4 tomatoes, peeled and chopped

juice of 1 lime

1 tbsp cider vinegar

2 tsp tomato paste

1 tsp fennel seeds

1 tsp mustard seeds

1 cup button mushrooms, quartered

2 oz fine beans, trimmed

1 zucchini, sliced

ground black pepper

basil sprig to garnish

NUTRITION FACTS	
Serving Size 1 (311g)	
Calories 127	Calories from Fat 18
	% Daily Value
Total Fat 2g	3%
Saturated Fat 0g	1%
Monounsaturated Fat 0.3g	0%
Polyunsaturated Fat 0.4g	0%
Cholesterol 0mg	0%
Sodium 516mg	22%
Total Carbohydrate 23g	8%
Dietary Fiber 2g	8%
Sugars 6g	0%
Protein 6g	0%

Percent daily values are based on a 2000 calorie diet

≈ Heat the broth in a large saucepan and cook the onion and garlic for 3–4 minutes. Add the wine, tomatoes, lime juice, vinegar, tomato paste, fennel, and mustard seeds and the vegetables. Bring the mixture to a boil, reduce the heat and simmer for 20 minutes or until the vegetables are just cooked. Season with black pepper to taste.

≈ Transfer the mixture to a serving dish, cover and chill for at least 1 hour. Garnish with basil and serve.

PUMPKIN SOUP

SERVES 4

A filling soup, thickened with potato, this dish would also suffice as a light snack. Canned pumpkin is used for speed and ease.

≈ Place the onion, broth, potatoes, and corn in a large pan. Cook for 15 minutes until the potatoes are tender.

≈ Add the canned pumpkin, milk, and half of the chives. Cook for 5 minutes. Ladle into serving bowls, sprinkle with the remaining chives and serve.

1 small onion, chopped

2 cups vegetable broth

6 oz potatoes, diced

1⅓ cups drained, canned corn kernels

1 lb can of pumpkin

1¼ cups skim milk

2 tbsp fresh snipped chives

NUTRITION FACTS	
Serving Size 1 (426g)	
Calories 187	Calories from Fat 18
	% Daily Value
Total Fat 2g	3%
Saturated Fat 1g	3%
Monounsaturated Fat 0.6g	0%
Polyunsaturated Fat 0.5g	0%
Cholesterol 1mg	0%
Sodium 657mg	27%
Total Carbohydrate 37g	12%
Dietary Fiber 6g	23%
Sugars 6g	0%
Protein 9g	0%

Percent daily values are based on a 2000 calorie diet

BROILED ENDIVE PEARS

SERVES 6

Endive has a slightly bitter flavor which is complemented perfectly by the sweetness of the pears in this recipe. Prepare and cook this dish just before serving as the endive browns quickly if cut and allowed to stand.

≈ Cut the endive heads in half lengthwise. Mix half of the oil with the garlic and brush all over the endive. Cook under a hot broiler for 3–4 minutes or until the endive begins to color. Turn the endive halves over and cook for a further 1–2 minutes.

≈ Carefully turn the endive again and top each piece with the sliced pear. Mix the remaining oil with the lemon juice and thyme, season and brush over the pears and endive. Cook under the hot broiler for 3–4 minutes until the pears begin to color, and transfer to warmed serving plates. Scatter the chestnuts over the top and spoon the lemon juice onto the pears. Sprinkle with lemon zest and garnish with fresh thyme sprigs. Serve immediately with hot crusty bread.

4 small heads of endive

4 tsp sunflower oil

1 garlic clove, minced

2 ripe dessert pears, halved, cored, and sliced

1 tbsp lemon juice

2 tsp fresh chopped thyme

ground black pepper

2 oz peeled chestnuts, cooked and chopped

lemon juice, lemon rind, and thyme sprigs to serve

NUTRITION FACTS	
Serving Size 1 (106g)	
Calories 112	Calories from Fat 27
	% Daily Value
Total Fat 3g	5%
Saturated Fat 0g	2%
Monounsaturated Fat 1.5g	0%
Polyunsaturated Fat 1.3g	0%
Cholesterol 0mg	0%
Sodium 20mg	1%
Total Carbohydrate 20g	7%
Dietary Fiber 1g	6%
Sugars 8g	0%
Protein 1g	0%

Percent daily values are based on a 2000 calorie diet

LIGHT LUNCHES AND SUPPERS

Curried Lentil Pâté

Roasted Vegetables on Toast

Spinach Crêpes

Pasta Caponata

Chestnut Hash

Eggplant-stuffed Mushrooms

Spinach and Carrot Mousse

Vegetable Calzone

Stuffed Lettuce Leaves

Bean and Asparagus Fry

Garlic Eggplant Rolls

Chinese Noodles

CURRIED LENTIL PÂTÉ

SERVES 8

Red lentils are used for speed in this recipe as they do not require pre-soaking. Should you wish to use other lentils, wash and soak them well and cook before using in the recipe.

3 cups vegetable broth

1 onion, chopped

3 garlic cloves, minced

1 tsp ground cumin

1 tsp ground coriander

½ tsp chili powder

1 scant cup red split lentils, washed

1 egg

4 tbsp skim milk

2 tbsp peach relish

2 tbsp fresh chopped cilantro

ground black pepper

cilantro sprigs to garnish

≈ Heat ⅔ cup of the vegetable broth in a saucepan and cook the onion and garlic for 2–3 minutes or until the onion begins to soften. Add the ground cumin, ground coriander, chili powder, lentils, and the remaining broth. Bring the mixture to a boil, then reduce the heat and simmer for 20 minutes or until the lentils are soft and cooked. Remove the pan from the heat and drain well.

≈ Transfer the mixture to a food processor and add the egg, milk, relish, chopped cilantro, and black pepper to taste. Blend for 10 seconds until smooth. Spoon into a non-stick 2 lb loaf pan and smooth the surface with the back of a spoon. Cover and cook in the oven at 400°F for 1 hour or until firm to the touch.

≈ Allow the pâté to cool before transferring to the refrigerator to chill. Unmold the pâté, slice, garnish with cilantro, and serve with a crisp salad.

ROASTED VEGETABLES ON TOAST

SERVES 4

The flavor of roasted vegetables is quite different from that achieved by boiling or steaming, and one not to be missed. This Mediterranean mixture is really colorful and tastes great with the light cheese sauce.

≈ Heat the oven to 400°F. Blanch all of the vegetables in boiling water for 8 minutes and drain well. Transfer the vegetables to a roasting pan and sprinkle the oil and rosemary over the top. Cook in the oven for 25 minutes or until softened and beginning to char slightly.

≈ Meanwhile, heat the broth for the sauce in a pan with the milk. Add the garlic, cream cheese, ground black pepper, and mustard. Blend the corn-starch with 2 tablespoons of cold water to form a paste and stir into the sauce. Bring to a boil, stirring until thickened and add the rosemary.

≈ Cook the bread under the broiler for 2–3 minutes each side until golden. Arrange two slices of the toast on four warmed serving plates and top with the roast vegetables. Spoon on the sauce, garnish with basil and rosemary, and serve.

NUTRITION FACTS	
Serving Size 1 (139g)	
Calories 107	Calories from Fat 9
	% Daily Value
Total Fat 1g	2%
Saturated Fat 0g	1%
Monounsaturated Fat 0.3g	0%
Polyunsaturated Fat 0.2g	0%
Cholesterol 27mg	9%
Sodium 414mg	17%
Total Carbohydrate 17g	6%
Dietary Fiber 7g	28%
Sugars 4g	0%
Protein 8g	0%

Percent daily values are based on a 2000 calorie diet

1 head of fennel, trimmed and
    quartered

2 open cap flat mushrooms, peeled
    and sliced

1 zucchini, sliced

1 red bell pepper, seeded, halved,
    and sliced

1 red onion, cut into eight pieces

1 tbsp sunflower oil

2 rosemary sprigs

8 small slices of thick whole wheat
    bread

For the sauce

⅔ cup vegetable broth

⅓ cup skim milk

2 garlic cloves, minced

¼ cup low-fat cream cheese

ground black pepper

1 tsp Dijon mustard

1 tbsp cornstarch

1 rosemary sprig, chopped

basil and rosemary sprigs to garnish

Roasted Vegetables on Toast

NUTRITION FACTS	
Serving Size 1 (245g)	
Calories 250	Calories from Fat 72

	% Daily Value
Total Fat 8g	12%
Saturated Fat 1g	4%
Monounsaturated Fat 1.9g	0%
Polyunsaturated Fat 1.5g	0%
Cholesterol 9mg	3%
Sodium 430mg	18%
Total Carbohydrate 43g	14%
Dietary Fiber 7g	28%
Sugars 3g	0%
Protein 13g	0%

Percent daily values are based on a 2000 calorie diet

SPINACH CRÊPES

SERVES 4

*These unusual light crêpes are made from a low-fat dough and rolled out.
Keep an eye on them during cooking as they can quickly brown.*

≈ Sift the flour for the crêpes into a mixing bowl and make a well in the center. Heat the water and oil to boiling point and pour into the flour, mixing to form a dough. Turn onto a floured surface and knead for 3–4 minutes.

≈ Cut the mixture into four equal portions and roll each into a 6-inch round. Heat a heavy, non-stick skillet over a medium heat. Put one of the crêpes into the pan and place another on top. Cook for 3–4 minutes, turning once when the bottom crêpe begins to brown. Cover the cooked crêpes with a clean, damp dish towel and repeat with remaining mixture. Cover and reserve.

≈ Heat the broth for the filling in a saucepan and cook the vegetables, garlic, and nutmeg for 7–8 minutes, stirring. Drain the mixture well.

≈ Blend 2 tablespoons of the milk for the sauce to a paste with the cornstarch. Put in a saucepan with the remaining milk, vegetable broth, seasoning, thyme, and half of the cheese. Bring the mixture to a boil, stirring until thickened.

≈ Heat the oven to 375°F. Spoon the vegetable mixture onto one half of each crêpe and roll up. Put in a shallow oven-proof dish, seam side down. Pour the sauce over the top and sprinkle with the remaining cheese and paprika. Cook in the oven for 15 minutes until golden brown. Serve immediately with salad.

For the crêpes

¾ cup all-purpose flour

½ cup water

1 tsp sunflower oil

For the filling

2 tbsp vegetable broth

1 small zucchini, sliced

1 cup spinach, shredded

1 small onion, chopped

1 cup button mushrooms, sliced

½ red bell pepper, seeded and cut
     into strips

1 celery stalk, sliced

1 garlic clove, minced

a pinch of ground nutmeg

For the sauce

⅔ cup skim milk

1 tbsp cornstarch

⅔ cup vegetable broth

ground black pepper

1 tbsp fresh chopped thyme

½ cup low-fat vegetarian cheese,
     shredded

½ tsp paprika

NUTRITION FACTS	
Serving Size 1 (267g)	
Calories 174	Calories from Fat 27
	% Daily Value
Total Fat 3g	4%
Saturated Fat 0g	2%
Monounsaturated Fat 0.6g	0%
Polyunsaturated Fat 0.7g	0%
Cholesterol 1mg	0%
Sodium 390mg	16%
Total Carbohydrate 32g	11%
Dietary Fiber 2g	6%
Sugars 4g	0%
Protein 7g	0%

Percent daily values are based on a 2000 calorie diet

PASTA CAPONATA

SERVES 4

Caponata is a well-known tomato and vegetable dish which is perfect to serve hot as a low-fat pasta sauce. In this recipe dried penne has been used but any pasta shapes or noodles would work equally well.

1 large eggplant

salt

⅔ cup vegetable broth

1 onion, halved and sliced

2 garlic cloves, minced

2 cups plum tomatoes, chopped

2 tbsp cider vinegar

4 celery stalks, chopped

2 oz green beans, trimmed

¼ cup pitted green olives, halved

1 tbsp fresh chopped basil

ground black pepper

2 cups dried penne

basil sprigs to garnish

≈ Cut the eggplant into chunks and put in a colander. Sprinkle with salt and let stand for 20 minutes. Wash under cold water and pat dry. Cook the eggplant under a medium broiler for 5 minutes, turning until browned.

≈ Meanwhile, heat the broth in a saucepan and add the onion and garlic. Cook for 2–3 minutes until softened. Stir in the tomatoes, vinegar, celery, and beans. Cook over a gentle heat for 20 minutes, stirring occasionally. Add the eggplant, olives, and basil, season and cook for a further 10 minutes.

≈ Meanwhile, cook the penne in boiling salted water for 8–10 minutes or until just tender. Drain well and toss into the sauce. Spoon into a warmed serving dish, garnish with basil and serve.

NUTRITION FACTS	
Serving Size 1 (342g)	
Calories 324	Calories from Fat 27
	% Daily Value
Total Fat 3g	5%
Saturated Fat 0g	1%
Monounsaturated Fat 1.0g	0%
Polyunsaturated Fat 0.8g	0%
Cholesterol 0mg	0%
Sodium 333mg	14%
Total Carbohydrate 64g	21%
Dietary Fiber 5g	20%
Sugars 6g	0%
Protein 12g	0%

Percent daily values are based on a 2000 calorie diet

CHESTNUT HASH

SERVES 4

Cook the potatoes for this dish in advance or use up any leftover cooked potatoes for speed. Allow the potato to brown on the base of the pan for a crunchier texture.

1½ lb potatoes, peeled and cubed

1 red onion, halved and sliced

½ cup snow peas

½ cup broccoli florets

1 zucchini, sliced

1 green bell pepper, seeded and
  sliced

¼ cup drained, canned corn

2 garlic cloves, minced

1 tsp paprika

2 tbsp fresh chopped parsley

1¼ cups vegetable broth

⅓ cup chestnuts, cooked, peeled,
  and quartered

ground black pepper

parsley sprigs to garnish

NUTRITION FACTS	
Serving Size 1 (396g)	
Calories 247	Calories from Fat 9
	% Daily Value
Total Fat 1g	2%
Saturated Fat 0g	1%
Monounsaturated Fat 0.2g	0%
Polyunsaturated Fat 0.3g	0%
Cholesterol 0mg	0%
Sodium 431mg	18%
Total Carbohydrate 55g	18%
Dietary Fiber 5g	22%
Sugars 8g	0%
Protein 7g	0%

Percent daily values are based on a 2000 calorie diet

≈ Cook the potatoes in boiling water for 20 minutes or until softened. Drain well and reserve.

≈ Meanwhile, cook the remaining ingredients in a skillet for 10 minutes, stirring. Add the drained potatoes to the skillet and cook for a further 15 minutes, stirring and pressing down with the back of a spoon. Serve immediately with crusty bread.

EGGPLANT-STUFFED MUSHROOMS

SERVES 4

Make the eggplant purée in advance for this recipe and store in the refrigerator for up to one day.

1 eggplant

2 garlic cloves, minced

juice of 1 lime

1 cup whole wheat bread crumbs

1 tbsp tomato paste

1 tbsp fresh chopped cilantro

8 large open cap mushrooms, peeled

¼ cup low-fat vegetarian cheese, shredded

4 tbsp vegetable broth

cilantro sprigs to garnish

≈ Heat the oven to 425°F. Cut the eggplant in half lengthwise and place skin side uppermost in a baking dish. Cook in the oven for 30 minutes until soft. Remove the eggplant from the oven and allow to cool. Scoop the soft flesh from the skin and put in a food processor with the garlic and lime juice. Add the bread crumbs to the food processor with the tomato paste and cilantro and blend for 10 seconds to mix well.

≈ Spoon the purée onto the mushrooms pressing the mixture down. Sprinkle the cheese on top and transfer the mushrooms to a shallow ovenproof dish. Pour the broth around the mushrooms, cover and cook in the oven for 20 minutes. Remove the cover and cook for a further 5 minutes until golden on top.

≈ Remove the mushrooms from the oven and from the dish with a draining spoon. Serve with a mixed salad and garnish with cilantro.

NUTRITION FACTS	
Serving Size 1 (128g)	
Calories 161	Calories from Fat 27
	% Daily Value
Total Fat 3g	5%
Saturated Fat 1g	3%
Monounsaturated Fat 1.4g	0%
Polyunsaturated Fat 0.7g	0%
Cholesterol 0mg	0%
Sodium 389mg	16%
Total Carbohydrate 27g	9%
Dietary Fiber 3g	12%
Sugars 1g	0%
Protein 6g	0%

Percent daily values are based on a 2000 calorie diet

SPINACH AND CARROT MOUSSE

SERVES 8

This is an impressive dish which is deceiving as it is so simple. It is ideal for entertaining as it may be made in advance and chilled.

1 lb spinach, stalks removed

1 tsp ground ginger

1 tsp curry powder

1 onion, chopped

3 cups carrots, shredded

2 garlic cloves, minced

4 tbsp vegetable broth

4 egg whites

shredded zucchini to garnish

≈ Wash the spinach and cook, covered, in a large saucepan on a low heat for 5 minutes until wilted. Drain very well, squeezing out as much liquid as possible and blend in a food processor with the ginger and curry powder for 10 seconds. Transfer the purée to a mixing bowl.

≈ Cook the onion, carrots, and garlic in the broth for 10 minutes or until the carrots are soft. Put in a food processor and blend for 10 seconds. Transfer to a separate mixing bowl.

≈ Whisk the egg whites until peaking and fold half into each of the vegetable purées. Spoon half of the carrot mixture into the base of a non-stick 2 lb loaf pan, top with half of the spinach mixture and repeat once more. Cover and stand in a roasting pan half filled with boiling water.

≈ Heat the oven to 350°F. Cook the mousse for 1 hour or until set. Leave to cool and then transfer to the fridge to chill completely. Turn the mousse onto a serving plate, arrange zucchini strips around the base and serve.

VEGETABLE CALZONE

SERVES 4

Calzone or pizza dough pasties are perfect for filling with your favorite ingredients. In this recipe the dough is slightly sweetened with honey for added flavor, but seeds or herbs could be added to the dough, or even garlic for variety.

NUTRITION FACTS	
Serving Size 1 (166g)	
Calories 49	Calories from Fat 9
	% Daily Value
Total Fat 1g	1%
Saturated Fat 0g	0%
Monounsaturated Fat 0.0g	0%
Polyunsaturated Fat 0.1g	0%
Cholesterol 0mg	0%
Sodium 208mg	9%
Total Carbohydrate 6g	2%
Dietary Fiber 3g	13%
Sugars 1g	0%
Protein 7g	0%

Percent daily values are based on a 2000 calorie diet

≈ Sift the flour for the dough into a large mixing bowl. Add the yeast and make a well in the center. Stir in the honey and broth and bring together to a dough. Turn the dough onto a lightly floured surface and knead for 10 minutes until smooth and elastic. Put in a mixing bowl, cover, and leave in a warm place to rise for 1 hour or until doubled in size.

≈ Meanwhile, heat the broth for the filling in a saucepan and stir in the tomatoes, basil, garlic, tomato paste, celery, and leek and cook for 5 minutes, stirring.

≈ Divide the risen dough into four equal pieces. Roll each out on a lightly floured surface to a circle 7 inches in diameter. Spoon equal amounts of the filling onto one half of each dough circle. Sprinkle with cheese. Brush the edge with milk and fold the dough over to form four semi-circles. Crimp the seams, pressing together to seal and transfer the calzone to a non-stick baking sheet. Brush with milk.

≈ Heat the oven to 425°F. Cook the calzone for 30 minutes until risen and golden. Serve with salad.

Vegetable Calzone

For the dough

4 cups white bread flour

1 tsp easy-blend dried yeast

1 tbsp clear honey

1¼ cups vegetable broth

skim milk for glazing

For the filling

½ cup vegetable broth

⅔ cup sundried tomatoes, chopped

2 tbsp fresh chopped basil

2 garlic cloves, minced

2 tbsp tomato paste

1 celery stalk, sliced

1 leek, sliced

¼ cup low-fat vegetarian cheese, shredded

NUTRITION FACTS	
Serving Size 1 (332g)	
Calories 584	Calories from Fat 45

	% Daily Value
Total Fat 5g	8%
Saturated Fat 0g	2%
Monounsaturated Fat 0.4g	0%
Polyunsaturated Fat 0.5g	0%
Cholesterol 0mg	0%
Sodium 653mg	27%
Total Carbohydrate 114g	38%
Dietary Fiber 3g	13%
Sugars 9g	0%
Protein 25g	0%

Percent daily values are based on a 2000 calorie diet

STUFFED LETTUCE LEAVES

SERVES 4

These small lettuce parcels are packed with a spicy vegetable and rice filling, then baked with a tomato sauce for a complete meal in itself. Make the filling and the sauce in advance and assemble the dish just before required. The recipe would also adequately serve eight as an appetizer, with only one parcel per person.

1¼ cups vegetable broth

1 red onion, chopped

2 garlic cloves, minced

1 cup button mushrooms, chopped

¼ cup brown rice

⅓ cup drained, canned corn

1 tsp curry powder

8 large, firm lettuce leaves such as
    iceberg or romaine

For the sauce

2 cups puréed tomatoes

1 tsp light soy sauce

½ tsp chili sauce

1 tbsp fresh chopped basil

1 tsp light brown sugar

ground black pepper

≈ Heat 5 tablespoons of the vegetable broth in a saucepan, add the onion and garlic and cook for 3–4 minutes until the onion begins to soften. Stir in the mushrooms, rice, corn, curry powder, and remaining broth, bring to a boil, reduce the heat and simmer for 30–40 minutes until the rice is cooked and the liquid has been absorbed.

≈ Meanwhile, mix all of the sauce ingredients in a pan and bring to a boil. Reduce the heat, cover, and simmer for 10 minutes.

≈ Heat the oven to 350°F. Place the lettuce leaves on a chopping board and spoon equal quantities of the rice filling into the center of each. Wrap the leaves around the filling and place seam side down in an ovenproof dish. Spoon the sauce over the top and cook in the oven for 10 minutes. Serve immediately.

BEAN AND ASPARAGUS FRY

SERVES 4

Fresh green beans and tender young asparagus are complemented in this recipe by a honey and lime-based sauce. Use any mixture of green beans that you have to hand for a quick and delicious dish.

≈ Top and tail the beans and cut into 1-inch slices, if necessary. Mix the beans and asparagus together.

≈ Heat the broth in a large skillet and add the vegetables, honey, lime juice, pepper, garlic, fennel seeds, and mustard. Cook, stirring for 7–8 minutes until the vegetables are cooked but crisp. Stir in the cheese and parsley and serve immediately.

NUTRITION FACTS	
Serving Size 1 (288g)	
Calories 87	Calories from Fat 9
	% Daily Value
Total Fat 1g	1%
Saturated Fat 0g	0%
Monounsaturated Fat 0.1g	0%
Polyunsaturated Fat 0.2g	0%
Cholesterol 0mg	0%
Sodium 771mg	32%
Total Carbohydrate 19g	6%
Dietary Fiber 2g	6%
Sugars 6g	0%
Protein 3g	0%

Percent daily values are based on a 2000 calorie diet

8 oz mixed fresh beans (e.g. green,
      wax, or fine beans)

8 oz young asparagus spears

⅔ cup shelled lima beans

½ cup vegetable broth

2 tbsp clear honey

1 tbsp lime juice

ground black pepper

3 garlic cloves, minced

1 tsp fennel seeds

1 tsp Dijon mustard

¼ cup low-fat vegetarian cheese,
      shredded

2 tbsp fresh chopped parsley

Bean and Asparagus Fry

NUTRITION FACTS	
Serving Size 1 (196g)	
Calories 295	Calories from Fat 27

	% Daily Value
Total Fat 3g	5%
Saturated Fat 0g	2%
Monounsaturated Fat 1.0g	0%
Polyunsaturated Fat 1.0g	0%
Cholesterol 0mg	0%
Sodium 509mg	21%
Total Carbohydrate 53g	18%
Dietary Fiber 10g	39%
Sugars 12g	0%
Protein 18g	0%

Percent daily values are based on a 2000 calorie diet

GARLIC EGGPLANT ROLLS

SERVES 8

These may take a little preparation but they are well worth the effort. Cooking garlic in its skin takes away the strong flavor and produces a milder garlic purée. This can be cooked in advance with the eggplant and gently warmed through to make the rolls.

8 garlic cloves

1 eggplant, sliced

1 tbsp sunflower oil

½ cup sundried tomatoes, reconstituted and sliced

2 tbsp basil leaves, shredded

4 lettuce leaves, shredded

4 ciabatta or crusty large rolls

≈ Heat the oven to 400°F. Put the garlic and eggplant slices on a nonstick baking sheet and cook in the oven for 30 minutes until soft. Remove from the oven and cool.

≈ Squeeze the garlic purée from the cloves and reserve. Mix the tomatoes, basil, and lettuce leaves together. Heat the rolls in a warm oven for 2–3 minutes and slice in half. Spread the garlic purée onto one half of each roll and top with the eggplant slices. Add the tomato mixture and top with remaining roll halves. Serve hot.

NUTRITION FACTS	
Serving Size 1 (83g)	
Calories 132	Calories from Fat 27
	% Daily Value
Total Fat 3g	5%
Saturated Fat 0g	2%
Monounsaturated Fat 1.3g	0%
Polyunsaturated Fat 0.2g	0%
Cholesterol 0mg	0%
Sodium 166mg	7%
Total Carbohydrate 23g	8%
Dietary Fiber 1g	5%
Sugars 0g	0%
Protein 4g	0%

Percent daily values are based on a 2000 calorie diet

CHINESE NOODLES

SERVES 4

This is a really quick and easy dish for a speedy lunch or supper. Use egg or rice noodles for a Chinese flavor or pasta ribbons if preferred, but these will require cooking for 8–10 minutes.

8 oz thin egg or rice noodles

⅓ cup vegetable broth

2 garlic cloves, minced

1 red onion, halved and sliced

1 in piece of ginger root, shredded

1 red chile, chopped

2 carrots, cut into strips

¾ cup snap peas

1 zucchini, sliced

1 celery stalk, sliced

1 tsp curry powder

3 tbsp dark soy sauce

3 tbsp plum sauce

1 tsp fennel seeds

fresh chopped parsley or fennel
    leaves to garnish

≈ Cook the noodles in boiling water for 3 minutes. Drain and reserve. Meanwhile, heat the broth in a nonstick wok or skillet and cook the vegetables and spices for 3–4 minutes, stirring constantly.

≈ Add the drained noodles to the pan with the soy and plum sauces and the fennel seeds. Cook for 2–3 minutes, tossing well and serve garnished with parsley or fennel leaves.

NUTRITION FACTS	
Serving Size 1 (265g)	
Calories 139	Calories from Fat 9
	% Daily Value
Total Fat 1g	1%
Saturated Fat 0g	1%
Monounsaturated Fat 0.2g	0%
Polyunsaturated Fat 0.1g	0%
Cholesterol 0mg	0%
Sodium 1004mg	42%
Total Carbohydrate 31g	10%
Dietary Fiber 4g	14%
Sugars 9g	0%
Protein 4g	0%

Percent daily values are based on a 2000 calorie diet

Classic Vegetable Dishes and Casseroles

Vegetable Lasagne

Vegetable and Tofu Pie

Mixed Bean Chili

Vegetable Flan

Stuffed Pasta Shells

Wild Rice and Lentil Casserole

Spicy Garbanzo Beans

Winter Vegetable Casserole

Roast Pepper Tart

Pasta Timbale

Saffron Rice and Vegetables

Vegetable Pilaf

Vegetable Risotto

Vegetable Chop Suey

Tofu Burgers and Fries

VEGETABLE LASAGNE

SERVES 4

This is a low fat version of a classic dish using a colorful mixture of vegetables to replace the meat. Serve with salad for a delicious combination.

1 small eggplant

salt

16 oz can chopped tomatoes

2 garlic cloves, minced

1 tbsp chopped basil

1 large zucchini, seeded and chopped

1 onion, chopped

1 green bell pepper, seeded and chopped

1 cup button mushrooms, sliced

1 tsp chili powder

ground black pepper

4 oz lasagne verdi (no pre-cook variety)

For the sauce

⅔ cup vegetable broth

1¼ cups skim milk

½ cup low fat vegetarian cheese, shredded

1 tsp Dijon mustard

2 tbsp cornstarch

1 tbsp fresh chopped basil

≈ Slice the eggplant and put in a colander. Sprinkle with salt and leave for 30 minutes. Wash and pat dry.

≈ Put the tomatoes, garlic, basil, zucchini, onion, bell pepper, mushrooms and chili powder in a saucepan. Add the eggplant and cook for 30 minutes, stirring occasionally until the vegetables are cooked.

≈ Mix the broth for the sauce, the milk, half of the cheese and the mustard in a saucepan. Blend the cornstarch with

4 tablespoons cold water to form a paste and add to the pan. Bring to a boil, stirring until thickened.

≈ Spoon a layer of the vegetable mixture into the base of an ovenproof dish. Lay half of the lasagne on top to cover. Spoon on remaining vegetable mixture and cover with the remaining lasagne. Pour the cheese sauce over the top and cook in the oven at 375°F for 40 minutes or until golden and bubbling. Sprinkle the basil on top and serve.

VEGETABLE AND TOFU PIE

SERVES 8

In this recipe, firm tofu (bean curd) is cubed and added to the pie. If liked, use a marinated tofu for extra flavor and use in the same way.

≈ Place all of the vegetables and the tofu in a non-stick skillet and dry fry for 3–5 minutes, stirring. Add the broth and cilantro, season and cook for 20 minutes or until the vegetables are tender. Blend the cornstarch to a paste with 2 tablespoons of cold water, add to the mixture and bring the mixture to a boil, stirring until thickened.

≈ Spoon the mixture into an ovenproof pie dish. Lay one sheet of filo pastry on top and brush with melted fat. Cut the remaining pastry into strips and lay on top, folding as you go to create a rippled effect. Sprinkle the remaining fat on top and cook the pie in the oven at 400°F for 20 minutes until golden brown.

≈ Serve with new potatoes.

NUTRITION FACTS	
Serving Size 1 (401g)	
Calories 264	Calories from Fat 45
	% Daily Value
Total Fat 5g	7%
Saturated Fat 0g	2%
Monounsaturated Fat 1.7g	0%
Polyunsaturated Fat 0.9g	0%
Cholesterol 1mg	0%
Sodium 306mg	13%
Total Carbohydrate 45g	15%
Dietary Fiber 5g	19%
Sugars 10g	0%
Protein 13g	0%

Percent daily values are based on a 2000 calorie diet

4 sheets of filo pastry

1 tbsp polyunsaturated low-fat
  spread, melted

For the filling

1 leek, sliced

2 garlic cloves, minced

2 carrots, diced

1 cup cauliflower florets

4 oz fine beans, halved

2 celery stalks, sliced

8 oz firm tofu, diced

1¼ cups vegetable broth

2 tbsp fresh chopped cilantro

ground black pepper

1 tbsp cornstarch

Vegetable and Tofu Pie

NUTRITION FACTS	
Serving Size 1 (152g)	
Calories 130	Calories from Fat 27
	% Daily Value
Total Fat 3g	4%
Saturated Fat 0g	2%
Monounsaturated Fat 0.6g	0%
Polyunsaturated Fat 1.3g	0%
Cholesterol 0mg	0%
Sodium 257mg	11%
Total Carbohydrate 21g	7%
Dietary Fiber 1g	5%
Sugars 3g	0%
Protein 7g	0%

Percent daily values are based on a 2000 calorie diet

MIXED BEAN CHILI

SERVES 4

Chili con carne has always been a warming favorite, and this recipe without the "carne" is no exception. Packed with vegetables and beans, it is a fully satisfying meal.

16 oz canned beans such as borlotti, red kidney, black eye and pinto beans, drained

14 oz can chopped tomatoes

1 tbsp tomato paste

1 onion, halved and sliced

⅔ cup potatoes, cubed

1 green bell pepper, seeded and chopped

¾ cup baby corn, halved

2 green chiles, seeded and chopped

1 tsp chili powder

2 garlic cloves, crushed

⅔ cup vegetable broth

fresh chopped parsley to garnish

NUTRITION FACTS	
Serving Size 1 (351g)	
Calories 178	Calories from Fat 9
	% Daily Value
Total Fat 1g	2%
Saturated Fat 0g	1%
Monounsaturated Fat 0.2g	0%
Polyunsaturated Fat 0.3g	0%
Cholesterol 0mg	0%
Sodium 808mg	34%
Total Carbohydrate 36g	12%
Dietary Fiber 7g	30%
Sugars 5g	0%
Protein 8g	0%

Percent daily values are based on a 2000 calorie diet

≈ Place all of the ingredients except the garnish in a large saucepan and bring to a boil. Reduce the heat, cover the pan and simmer for 45 minutes or until all of the vegetables are cooked and the juices have thickened slightly. Stir the chili occasionally while cooking.

≈ Garnish with parsley and serve with brown rice or baked potatoes.

VEGETABLE FLAN

SERVES 4

This flan is made with a low-fat pastry which is flavored with mustard. Although it is not quite as short as a traditional pastry it is delicious hot when filled with vegetables and low-fat cheese.

For the pastry

1 cup flour

2 tbsp skim milk

1½ tsp baking powder

1 tsp mustard powder

For the filling

1 celery stalk, sliced

¾ cup button mushrooms, sliced

2 baby corn cobs, sliced

1 leek, sliced

2 garlic cloves, minced

8 asparagus spears, trimmed

½ cup vegetable broth

½ cup low-fat cottage cheese

⅔ cup skim milk

1 egg white, beaten

≈ Heat the oven to 400°F. Mix the pastry ingredients in a bowl and add enough cold water to bring the mixture together to form a soft dough. Roll the pastry out on a lightly floured surface to fit an 8-inch pie dish.

≈ Cook the prepared vegetables in the broth for 5 minutes, stirring. Remove from the pan with a draining spoon and place in a bowl. Add the cottage cheese, milk and egg white. Spoon the mixture into the pastry case and cook for 40 minutes until set and golden brown. Serve hot with salad.

NUTRITION FACTS	
Serving Size 1 (256g)	
Calories 207	Calories from Fat 18
	% Daily Value
Total Fat 2g	3%
Saturated Fat 0g	2%
Monounsaturated Fat 0.2g	0%
Polyunsaturated Fat 0.3g	0%
Cholesterol 2mg	1%
Sodium 506mg	21%
Total Carbohydrate 37g	12%
Dietary Fiber 2g	7%
Sugars 6g	0%
Protein 12g	0%

Percent daily values are based on a 2000 calorie diet

STUFFED PASTA SHELLS

SERVES 4

These large pasta shells are ideal for filling and serving with a sauce. Quick to cook, they look fabulous and are great for entertaining.

16 large pasta shells

For the sauce

16 oz can chopped tomatoes

2 garlic cloves, minced

1 tbsp fresh chopped parsley

1 onion, chopped

2 tbsp tomato paste

ground black pepper

For the filling

4 tbsp vegetable broth

1 zucchini, diced

¼ cup canned or frozen corn kernels

1 green bell pepper, seeded and ·diced

¾ cup button mushrooms, sliced

1 leek, sliced

2 garlic cloves, minced

1 tbsp fresh chopped mixed herbs

basil sprigs to garnish

≈ Place the sauce ingredients in a pan, bring to a boil, cover, and simmer for 10 minutes. Transfer to a food processor and blend for 10 seconds. Return the sauce to the pan and heat through.
≈ Meanwhile, put all of the filling ingredients, except the herbs, in a saucepan and cook for 10 minutes, simmering until the vegetables are tender. Stir in the herbs and season.

≈ Cook the pasta in boiling salted water for 8–10 minutes until just tender, drain well. Spoon the vegetable filling into the pasta shells and arrange on warmed serving plates. Spoon the sauce around the shells, garnish with basil and serve.

WILD RICE AND LENTIL CASSEROLE

SERVES 4

This dish is superb on a cold day as it is really hearty and warming. To check that the rice is cooked, look at the ends to be sure they have split open, otherwise cook for a little longer until it is visibly cooked through.

≈ Cook the lentils and wild rice in the vegetable broth in a large flameproof casserole dish for 20 minutes, stirring occasionally.

≈ Add the onion, garlic, tomatoes, spices, mushrooms, bell pepper, broccoli, and corn. Bring the mixture to a boil, reduce the heat and cook for a further 15 minutes until the rice and lentils are cooked. Add the chopped cilantro, garnish and serve with warm crusty bread.

NUTRITION FACTS	
Serving Size 1 (251g)	
Calories 82	Calories from Fat 9
	% Daily Value
Total Fat 1g	2%
Saturated Fat 0g	1%
Monounsaturated Fat 0.19g	0%
Polyunsaturated Fat 0.3g	0%
Cholesterol 0mg	0%
Sodium 461mg	19%
Total Carbohydrate 18g	6%
Dietary Fiber 3g	13%
Sugars 7g	0%
Protein 3g	0%

Percent daily values are based on a 2000 calorie diet

Wild Rice and Lentil Casserole

scant cup red split lentils

⅓ cup wild rice

4 cups vegetable broth

1 red onion, cut into eight pieces

2 garlic cloves, minced

14 oz can chopped tomatoes

1 tsp ground coriander

1 tsp ground cumin

1 tsp chili powder

salt and ground black pepper

2½ cups button mushrooms, sliced

1 green bell pepper, seeded and
    sliced

1 cup broccoli florets

¾ cup baby corn cobs, halved

1 tbsp fresh chopped cilantro

cilantro sprigs to garnish

NUTRITION FACTS	
Serving Size 1 (593g)	
Calories 242	Calories from Fat 27
	% Daily Value
Total Fat 3g	4%
Saturated Fat 0g	1%
Monounsaturated Fat 0.2g	0%
Polyunsaturated Fat 0.5g	0%
Cholesterol 0mg	0%
Sodium 1384mg	58%
Total Carbohydrate 43g	14%
Dietary Fiber 16g	66%
Sugars 7g	0%
Protein 18g	0%

Percent daily values are based on a 2000 calorie diet

SPICY GARBANZO BEANS

SERVES 4

Garbanzo beans are a great source of carbohydrate and are important in a vegetarian diet. Here they are simmered in a spicy tomato sauce and are delicious served with brown rice.

1 cup garbanzo beans

1 tsp baking soda

1 onion, halved and sliced

1 inch piece of ginger root, shredded

4 tomatoes, chopped

1 green chile, chopped

1 tsp curry powder

½ tsp chili powder

1 tsp ground coriander

1¼ cups vegetable broth

fresh chopped cilantro to garnish

NUTRITION FACTS	
Serving Size 1 (274g)	
Calories 250	Calories from Fat 36
	% Daily Value
Total Fat 4g	6%
Saturated Fat 1g	5%
Monounsaturated Fat 1.4g	0%
Polyunsaturated Fat 0.9g	0%
Cholesterol 4mg	1%
Sodium 709mg	30%
Total Carbohydrate 42g	14%
Dietary Fiber 4g	15%
Sugars 7g	0%
Protein 14g	0%

Percent daily values are based on a 2000 calorie diet

≈ Put the garbanzo beans in a large mixing bowl with the baking soda and enough water to cover. Leave to soak overnight. Drain the garbanzo beans and cover with fresh water in a large saucepan. Bring to a boil and boil rapidly for 10 minutes. Reduce the heat and simmer for 1 hour or until cooked.

≈ Drain the garbanzo beans and put in a nonstick skillet with the remaining ingredients. Cover and simmer for 20 minutes, stirring occasionally. Garnish with cilantro and serve with brown rice.

WINTER VEGETABLE CASSEROLE

SERVES 4

This recipe makes use of many winter vegetables, but use whatever you have to hand as long as there is a good mixture. Cauliflower helps to thicken the sauce slightly, therefore it is always best to include this in your recipe.

2 large potatoes, sliced

3¾ cups vegetable broth

2 carrots, cut into chunks

1 onion, sliced

2 garlic cloves, minced

2 parsnips, cored and sliced

1 leek, sliced

2 celery stalks, sliced

1½ cups cauliflower florets

salt and ground black pepper

1 tsp paprika

2 tbsp fresh chopped mixed herbs

¼ cup low-fat vegetarian cheese, shredded

≈ Cook the potatoes in boiling water for 10 minutes. Drain well and reserve. Meanwhile, heat 1¼ cups of the broth in a flameproof casserole dish. Add all of the vegetables, remaining broth, seasoning, and paprika and cook for 15 minutes stirring occasionally. Add the herbs and adjust the seasoning.

≈ Lay the potato slices on top of the vegetable mixture and sprinkle the cheese on top. Cook in the oven at 375°F for 30 minutes or until the top is golden brown and the cheese has melted. Serve with a salad.

NUTRITION FACTS	
Serving Size 1 (479g)	
Calories 180	Calories from Fat 27
	% Daily Value
Total Fat 3g	5%
Saturated Fat 0g	1%
Monounsaturated Fat 0.8g	0%
Polyunsaturated Fat 0.5g	0%
Cholesterol 0mg	0%
Sodium 1520mg	63%
Total Carbohydrate 35g	12%
Dietary Fiber 5g	22%
Sugars 9g	0%
Protein 8g	0%

Percent daily values are based on a 2000 calorie diet

ROAST PEPPER TART

SERVES 8

This is one of those dishes that is as appealing to the eye as to the palate. A medley of roast peppers in a cheese sauce are served in a crisp filo pastry shell. For a dinner party, make individual pastry shells and serve the tarts with a small salad.

8 oz filo pastry

1 cup margarine, melted

For the filling

2 red bell peppers, seeded and
    halved

2 green bell peppers, seeded and
    halved

2 garlic cloves, minced

For the sauce

1¼ cups skim milk

¼ cup low-fat vegetarian cheese,
    shredded

2 tbsp cornstarch

¼ cup vegetable broth

1 tbsp fresh snipped chives

1 tbsp fresh chopped basil

1 garlic clove, minced

1 tsp whole grain mustard

parsley sprigs to garnish

NUTRITION FACTS	
Serving Size 1 (150g)	
Calories 150	Calories from Fat 36
	% Daily Value
Total Fat 4g	6%
Saturated Fat 1g	3%
Monounsaturated Fat 1.4g	0%
Polyunsaturated Fat 1.5g	0%
Cholesterol 1mg	0%
Sodium 235mg	10%
Total Carbohydrate 23g	8%
Dietary Fiber 1g	2%
Sugars 2g	0%
Protein 5g	0%

Percent daily values are based on a 2000 calorie diet

≈ Lay two sheets of filo pastry in a pie plate allowing the pastry to overhang the sides a little. Brush with margarine and lay another two sheets on top at opposing angles. Brush with margarine and continue in this way until all of the pastry has been used. Heat the oven to 400°F and cook the pastry case for 15 minutes until golden and crisp.

≈ Meanwhile, lay the peppers on a baking sheet, skin side uppermost. Sprinkle the garlic over the peppers, cook in the oven for 20 minutes. Allow to cool slightly then peel the peppers, discarding the skin. Cut the peppers into strips and place in the pastry case.

≈ Heat the milk for the sauce in a pan, add the cheese and stir until melted. Blend the cornstarch with 4 tablespoons cold water to form a paste and stir, with the broth, into the sauce. Bring to a boil, stirring until thickened and add the remaining ingredients. Spoon the sauce over the peppers, garnish with basil and chives and serve.

PASTA TIMBALE

SERVES 8

This is a really different way to serve pasta in a zucchini-lined mold which is baked until set and served with a tomato sauce.

≈ Cut the zucchini into thin strips with a vegetable peeler and blanch in boiling water for 2–3 minutes. Refresh the zucchini under cold water, then put in a bowl and cover with cold water until required.

≈ Cook the pasta in boiling salted water for 8–10 minutes until just tender. Drain well and reserve.

≈ Heat the broth in a saucepan and cook the onions, garlic, carrot, corn, and bell pepper for 5 minutes. Stir in the pasta, cheese, tomatoes, eggs, and oregano, season well and cook for 3 minutes, stirring well.

≈ Line a 2 pt mold or round pan with the zucchini strips, covering the base and sides and allowing the strips to overhang the sides. Spoon the pasta mixture into the mold and fold the zucchini strips over the pasta to cover.

≈ Stand the mold in a roasting pan half filled with boiling water, cover, and cook in the oven at 350°F for 30–40 minutes until set.

≈ Meanwhile, put all of the sauce ingredients in a pan and bring to a boil, reduce the heat and cook for 10 minutes. Sieve the sauce into a clean pan and heat gently.

≈ Remove the pasta dish from the oven and carefully turn out of the mold onto a serving plate. Serve with the tomato sauce.

2 zucchini

1 cup pasta shapes such as macaroni or penne

6 tbsp vegetable broth

2 onions, chopped

2 garlic cloves, minced

1 carrot, chopped

2 tbsp drained, canned corn

1 green bell pepper, seeded and chopped

¼ cup low-fat vegetarian cheese, shredded

16 oz can chopped tomatoes

2 eggs, beaten

2 tbsp fresh chopped oregano

For the sauce

1 onion, chopped

1 lb tomatoes, chopped

2 tsp granulated sugar

2 tbsp tomato paste

¾ cup vegetable broth

NUTRITION FACTS	
Serving Size 1 (219g)	
Calories 100	Calories from Fat 27
	% Daily Value
Total Fat 3g	5%
Saturated Fat 1g	3%
Monounsaturated Fat 0.9g	0%
Polyunsaturated Fat 0.4g	0%
Cholesterol 58mg	19%
Sodium 451mg	19%
Total Carbohydrate 14g	5%
Dietary Fiber 2g	9%
Sugars 3g	0%
Protein 6g	0%

Percent daily values are based on a 2000 calorie diet

SAFFRON RICE AND VEGETABLES

SERVES 4

Basmati rice is grown in the foothills of the Himalayas. It is a narrow long-grain white rice, and one of the best to accompany spicy dishes such as this recipe.

For the rice

2½ cups vegetable broth

2 garlic cloves, minced

1 onion, sliced

scant cup basmati rice

a few strands of saffron

½ cup frozen peas

4 cardamom pods

3 cloves

1 bay leaf

1 tsp curry powder

For the vegetables

1¼ cups vegetable broth

1 onion, cut into eight pieces

3 garlic cloves

4 tomatoes, chopped

2 zucchini, sliced

1 potato, cubed

2 oz fine beans, trimmed and halved

1 tsp curry powder

1 tsp ground cumin

1 tsp ground coriander

1 tsp fennel seeds

⅔ cup low-fat plain yogurt

≈ Heat half of the broth for the rice in a saucepan and add the garlic, onion, rice, and saffron. Cook for 4 minutes, stirring. Add the remaining ingredients for the rice and bring to a boil. Reduce the heat to a simmer and cook for a further 20–30 minutes until the rice is cooked.

≈ Meanwhile, put all of the ingredients for the vegetables, except the yogurt, in a large saucepan and cook for 20 minutes, stirring occasionally until the vegetables are tender. Remove from the heat and stir in the yogurt. Serve with the spicy rice and bread.

VEGETABLE PILAF

SERVES 4

A pilaf is a spicy, fluffy rice. This recipe is packed with crisp vegetables, chestnuts, and raisins and lightly colored with saffron for a golden appearance. If you do not have saffron to hand, use a pinch of turmeric in its place.

≈ Heat the oil in a skillet and add the onion and rice. Cook for 3–4 minutes, stirring. Add the remaining ingredients and bring the mixture to a boil. Reduce the heat and cook for a further 30 minutes, stirring occasionally until the rice is cooked and the liquid absorbed.

≈ Mix together the sauce ingredients and serve with the pilaf and a side salad.

NUTRITION FACTS	
Serving Size 1 (710g)	
Calories 521	Calories from Fat 63
	% Daily Value
Total Fat 7g	10%
Saturated Fat 0g	2%
Monounsaturated Fat 0.3g	0%
Polyunsaturated Fat 0.4g	0%
Cholesterol 2mg	1%
Sodium 1053mg	44%
Total Carbohydrate 109g	36%
Dietary Fiber 15g	60%
Sugars 14g	0%
Protein 14g	0%

Percent daily values are based on a 2000 calorie diet

Vegetable Pilaf

2 tbsp sunflower oil

1 red onion, chopped

¾ cup basmati rice

a few strands of saffron

¼ cup corn kernels

1 red bell pepper, seeded and diced

1 tsp curry powder

1 tsp chili powder

1 green chile, seeded and chopped

1 cup broccoli florets

2½ cups vegetable broth

½ cup cooked and peeled chestnuts, halved

⅓ cup raisins

For the sauce

⅔ cup low-fat plain yogurt

2 tbsp fresh chopped mint

a pinch of cayenne pepper

NUTRITION FACTS	
Serving Size 1 (390g)	
Calories 379	Calories from Fat 90
	% Daily Value
Total Fat 10g	15%
Saturated Fat 1g	6%
Monounsaturated Fat 3.4g	0%
Polyunsaturated Fat 3.0g	0%
Cholesterol 2mg	1%
Sodium 781mg	33%
Total Carbohydrate 69g	23%
Dietary Fiber 5g	20%
Sugars 21g	0%
Protein 9g	0%

Percent daily values are based on a 2000 calorie diet

VEGETABLE RISOTTO

SERVES 4

Risotto is an Italian dish of cooked rice and either vegetables or meat. It has a creamy texture which is due to the special arborio risotto rice used. The recipe really does call for this but if you do not have any to hand it will still taste great with brown rice.

1½ tbsp polyunsaturated margarine

1 onion, halved and sliced

8 oz firm, lite tofu, cubed

generous cup arborio rice

½ tsp turmeric

1 tsp soy sauce

2½ cups vegetable broth

1 green chile, sliced

1 red bell pepper, seeded, halved, and sliced

⅓ cup snow peas

½ cup canned waterchestnuts, drained and halved

½ cup oyster mushrooms

NUTRITION FACTS	
Serving Size 1 (372g)	
Calories 182	Calories from Fat 54
	% Daily Value
Total Fat 6g	9%
Saturated Fat 1g	5%
Monounsaturated Fat 2.1g	0%
Polyunsaturated Fat 1.8g	0%
Cholesterol 0mg	0%
Sodium 911mg	38%
Total Carbohydrate 26g	9%
Dietary Fiber 1g	5%
Sugars 2g	0%
Protein 8g	0%

Percent daily values are based on a 2000 calorie diet

≈ Heat the margarine in a nonstick skillet and cook the onion and tofu for 3 minutes. Add the rice and turmeric and cook for a further 2 minutes.

≈ Add the soy sauce to the pan with the broth, chile, bell pepper, snow peas, and waterchestnuts. Bring the mixture to a boil, reduce the heat to a simmer and cook for 15–20 minutes until all of the vegetables are tender. Top the pan up with hot water or broth if required and stir frequently. Stir in the mushrooms and cook for 5 minutes and serve.

VEGETABLE CHOP SUEY

SERVES 4

Add a touch of China to your table with this simple recipe. Vegetables are cooked in a spiced soy sauce and served with brown rice for a quick and healthy meal.

≈ Pour the vegetable broth into a large skillet or wok with the Chinese five spice powder and cook all of the vegetables except the mushrooms and beansprouts for 5 minutes.

≈ Add the mushrooms, beansprouts and soy sauce to the pan and cook for a further 5 minutes, stirring well. Serve immediately with boiled brown rice.

1¼ cups vegetable broth

1 tsp Chinese five spice powder

3 carrots, cut into strips

3 celery stalks, sliced

1 red onion, sliced

1 green bell pepper, seeded and cut into chunks

½ cup open cap mushrooms, sliced

3 cups beansprouts

1 tbsp light soy sauce

NUTRITION FACTS	
Serving Size 1 (250g)	
Calories 57	Calories from Fat 9
	% Daily Value
Total Fat 1g	1%
Saturated Fat 0g	0%
Monounsaturated Fat 0.1g	0%
Polyunsaturated Fat 0.3g	0%
Cholesterol 0mg	0%
Sodium 620mg	26%
Total Carbohydrate 10g	3%
Dietary Fiber 3g	10%
Sugars 4g	0%
Protein 4g	0%

Percent daily values are based on a 2000 calorie diet

TOFU BURGERS AND FRIES

SERVES 4

Here is a recipe that low-fat dieters dream of. Although not fries in the strictest sense, these blanched potato sticks are tossed in flour and a little oil and baked to crispness in the oven.

≈ Boil the carrots in water for 10–12 minutes until soft. Drain really well. Cook the cabbage in boiling water for 5 minutes and drain really well. Put the carrots, cabbage, onion, tofu, and coriander in a food processor and blend for 10 seconds. Using floured hands form the mixture into four equal-sized burgers. Chill in the refrigerator for 1 hour or until firm.

≈ Cut the potatoes into thick fries and cook in boiling water for 10 minutes. Drain well and toss in the flour. Put the potatoes in a plastic bag and sprinkle in the oil. Seal the top of the bag and shake the fries to coat. Turn the potatoes out onto a nonstick baking sheet. Cook in the oven at 400°F for 30 minutes or until golden brown.

≈ Meanwhile, place the burgers under a hot broiler for 7–8 minutes, turning with a spatula. Toast the burger buns for 2 minutes and place a burger on one half. Add the tomatoes, lettuce, and onion and serve with the fries.

For the burgers

1 cup carrots, chopped

½ cup cabbage, shredded

1 onion, chopped

10 oz firm, lite tofu, cubed

1 tsp ground coriander

4 burger buns split

sliced tomatoes, lettuce, and onion

For the fries

2 large potatoes

2 tbsp flour

1 tbsp sunflower oil

NUTRITION FACTS	
Serving Size 1 (459g)	
Calories 280	Calories from Fat 63
	% Daily Value
Total Fat 7g	11%
Saturated Fat 1g	5%
Monounsaturated Fat 2.0g	0%
Polyunsaturated Fat 3.0g	0%
Cholesterol 0mg	0%
Sodium 218mg	9%
Total Carbohydrate 38g	13%
Dietary Fiber 5g	20%
Sugars 8g	0%
Protein 17g	0%

Percent daily values are based on a 2000 calorie diet

SEASONAL SIDE-DISH SELECTION

Trio of Purées

Potato and Cheese Layer

Herbed Cauliflower

Paprika Potato Salad

Stuffed Peppers

Minted Beans and Cucumber

Chestnut Brown Rice

Vegetable Gratinée

Spiced Eggplant

Steamed Honey-glazed Parsnips

Mixed Vegetable Dumplings

Sweet Red Cabbage

Caramelized Baked Onions

Hot Spicy Lentils

Three-Mushroom Fry

Ratatouille

Herb Gnocchi

Quick Spiced Rice

TRIO OF PURÉES

SERVES 4

These colorful vegetable purée molds are perfect for dinner parties. Alternatively, bake in one large ovenproof dish instead of individual molds.

10 oz potatoes, cubed

1 cup carrots, cubed

grated rind of 1 orange

1 tbsp orange juice

ground black pepper

8 oz sweet potato, cubed

dash of grated nutmeg

4 oz spinach

grated rind of 1 lemon

1 tbsp fresh chopped cilantro

≈ Cook the potatoes in boiling water for 20 minutes until soft. Drain and mash. Divide equally into three separate bowls.

≈ Boil the carrots for 10 minutes until soft. Drain and mash. Add to one bowl of potato with the orange rind and juice. Season with pepper.

≈ Cook the sweet potato for 10 minutes in boiling water. Drain and mash. Add to another bowl of potato with the nutmeg. Season with pepper.

≈ Blanch the spinach for 3 minutes in boiling water. Drain very well, pressing out all the moisture through a sieve. Add to the remaining bowl with the lemon rind and cilantro. Season with pepper.

≈ Place the contents of each bowl, separately, in a food processor and blend each for 1 minute. Repeat with each mixture. Spoon one-quarter of the carrot purée into the base of four lightly greased individual ramekin dishes. Top with one-quarter of the spinach mixture and finally spoon on one-quarter of the sweet potato mixture.

≈ Place the dishes in a roasting pan and fill with enough boiling water to come halfway up the sides. Cover and cook in the oven at 375°F for 1 hour. Remove the ramekins from the roasting pan. Turn out the purées onto serving plates. Serve with a main vegetable dish.

NUTRITION FACTS	
Serving Size 1 (189g)	
Calories 154	Calories from Fat 0
	% Daily Value
Total Fat 0g	1%
Saturated Fat 0g	0%
Monounsaturated Fat 0g	0%
Polyunsaturated Fat 0.1g	0%
Cholesterol 0mg	0%
Sodium 55mg	2%
Total Carbohydrate 35g	12%
Dietary Fiber 7g	27%
Sugars 10g	0%
Protein 4g	0%

Percent daily values are based on a 2000 calorie diet

POTATO AND CHEESE LAYER

SERVES 4

This recipe uses half fat cream substitute in place of full fat cream. If preferred, substitute with skim milk or vegetable broth.

1 lb potatoes, thinly sliced

2 garlic cloves, minced

½ cup low-fat cheese, shredded

1 onion, halved and sliced

2 tbsp fresh chopped parsley

½ cup half cream substitute

½ cup skim milk

ground black pepper

fresh chopped parsley to garnish

≈ Cook the potatoes in boiling water for 10 minutes. Drain well. Arrange a layer of potatoes in the base of a shallow ovenproof dish. Add a little garlic, cheese, onion, and parsley. Repeat the layers until all the potatoes, onion, cheese, garlic, and parsley are used, finishing with a layer of cheese.

≈ Mix together the half cream substitute and milk. Season and pour over the potato layers. Bake in the oven at 325°F for 1¼ hours until cooked through and golden brown. Garnish with parsley and serve.

NUTRITION FACTS	
Serving Size 1 (179g)	
Calories 159	Calories from Fat 9
	% Daily Value
Total Fat 1g	2%
Saturated Fat 0g	2%
Monounsaturated Fat 0.6g	0%
Polyunsaturated Fat 0.2g	0%
Cholesterol 1mg	0%
Sodium 44mg	2%
Total Carbohydrate 34g	11%
Dietary Fiber 3g	12%
Sugars 3g	0%
Protein 4g	0%

Percent daily values are based on a 2000 calorie diet

Potato and Cheese Layer ▶

HERBED CAULIFLOWER

SERVES 4

Cauliflower cheese traditionally has a rich cheese sauce coating the cauliflower. This low-fat version uses a wine and herb sauce which is equally delicious.

4 baby cauliflowers

2 mint sprigs

3¾ cups vegetable broth

¼ cup low-fat cheese, shredded

For the sauce

⅔ cup vegetable broth

1¼ cups skim milk

⅔ cup dry white wine

2 tbsp cornstarch

1 tbsp fresh chopped parsley

1 tbsp fresh chopped cilantro

1 tbsp fresh chopped thyme

ground black pepper

NUTRITION FACTS	
Serving Size 1 (846g)	
Calories 160	Calories from Fat 27

	% Daily Value
Total Fat 3g	4%
Saturated Fat 0g	2%
Monounsaturated Fat 0.1g	0%
Polyunsaturated Fat 0.0g	0%
Cholesterol 4mg	1%
Sodium 1309mg	55%
Total Carbohydrate 24g	8%
Dietary Fiber 12g	46%
Sugars 18g	0%
Protein 16g	0%

Percent daily values are based on a 2000 calorie diet

≈ Trim the cauliflowers and place in a large pan with the mint and broth. Cook gently for 10 minutes.

≈ Meanwhile, place the broth for the sauce, the milk, and white wine in a pan. Blend the cornstarch with 4 tablespoons of cold water and add to the pan. Bring to a boil, stirring, and add the herbs. Season and simmer for 2–3 minutes.

≈ Drain the cauliflower and place in an ovenproof dish. Pour on the sauce and top with the cheese. Broil for 2–3 minutes until the cheese has melted. Serve.

80

PAPRIKA POTATO SALAD

SERVES 4

This salad has a spicy Indian flavor. Perfect served accompanying either a spiced main dish or a green salad.

1 lb potatoes

½ cup vegetable broth

1 red onion, halved and sliced

¼ tsp ground cumin

1 green chile, chopped

¼ tsp ground turmeric

1 cardamom pod

1 tsp paprika

1 tomato, seeded and diced

1 tbsp fresh chopped parsley

≈ Cut the potatoes into 1-inch cubes. Cook in boiling water for 10 minutes. Drain well and reserve.

≈ Heat 3 tablespoons of the broth in a pan, add the onion and cook for 5 minutes until beginning to brown. Add the potatoes, cumin, chile, turmeric, cardamom pod, and paprika. Stir in the remaining broth and the tomato. Bring to a boil and cook for 5 minutes. Sprinkle with parsley and serve.

NUTRITION FACTS	
Serving Size 1 (219g)	
Calories 159	Calories from Fat 9
	% Daily Value
Total Fat 1g	1%
Saturated Fat 0g	0%
Monounsaturated Fat 0.0g	0%
Polyunsaturated Fat 0.2g	0%
Cholesterol 0mg	0%
Sodium 199mg	8%
Total Carbohydrate 35g	12%
Dietary Fiber 5g	22%
Sugars 4g	0%
Protein 4g	0%

Percent daily values are based on a 2000 calorie diet

STUFFED PEPPERS

SERVES 4

These peppers are filled with bulghar wheat flavored with cheese, vegetables, and fruit. Serve as an accompaniment or as a meal in themselves.

2/3 cup bulghar wheat

1 cup vegetable broth

4 red bell peppers

1/4 tsp ground turmeric

1/2 cup mushrooms, diced

2 tbsp dark raisins

2 tbsp dried apricots, diced

3 green onions, sliced

1/4 cup low-fat cheese, shredded

2 tbsp fresh chopped cilantro

1/4 tsp cayenne pepper

ground black pepper

≈ Place the bulghar wheat in a bowl and pour on the vegetable broth. Let sit for 30 minutes. Drain if required.

≈ Meanwhile, cut the tops from the peppers and remove the core and seeds. Cook the peppers in boiling water for 2 minutes, drain and refresh under cold water.

≈ Mix together the remaining ingredients. Stir into the bulghar wheat and spoon into the peppers. Season with black pepper.

≈ Stand the peppers in a shallow oven-proof dish and pour in enough boiling water to come halfway up the sides. Cover and cook in the oven at 350°F for 20 minutes. Serve.

NUTRITION FACTS

Serving Size 1 (268g)

Calories 209	Calories from Fat 9

	% Daily Value
Total Fat 1g	2%
Saturated Fat 0g	1%
Monounsaturated Fat 0.1g	0%
Polyunsaturated Fat 0.2g	0%
Cholesterol 2mg	1%
Sodium 274mg	11%
Total Carbohydrate 44g	15%
Dietary Fiber 8g	32%
Sugars 3g	0%
Protein 8g	0%

Percent daily values are based on a 2000 calorie diet

MINTED BEANS AND CUCUMBER

SERVES 4

Cucumber is not usually served hot, but it is cooked perfectly with the beans in this recipe and delicately flavored with mint. An unusual but delicious side dish.

1 lb fine beans, trimmed

1/2 cucumber, thickly sliced

2 garlic cloves, minced

4 mint sprigs

1 tbsp lemon juice

1/3 cup vegetable broth

ground black pepper

strips of lemon rind for garnish

≈ Prepare the vegetables and place on a large sheet of foil. Bring up the sides of the foil around the vegetables and crimp to form an open package. Add the remaining ingredients, season and seal the top of the package.

≈ Place the package in a steamer and cook for 25 minutes or until the beans are tender. Garnish and serve.

NUTRITION FACTS

Serving Size 1 (185g)

Calories 40	Calories from Fat 9

	% Daily Value
Total Fat 1g	2%
Saturated Fat 0g	1%
Monounsaturated Fat 0.4g	0%
Polyunsaturated Fat 0.3g	0%
Cholesterol 0mg	0%
Sodium 106mg	4%
Total Carbohydrate 6g	2%
Dietary Fiber 2g	9%
Sugars 3g	0%
Protein 2g	0%

Percent daily values are based on a 2000 calorie diet

Minted Beans and Cucumber ▶

CHESTNUT BROWN RICE

SERVES 4

Chestnuts are one of the few nuts that are not very high in fat. They add to the nutty flavor of the rice in this recipe.

3¾ cups vegetable broth

generous cup brown rice

1 red onion, halved and sliced

2 garlic cloves, minced

4 oz cooked chestnuts, quartered

2 celery stalks, sliced

3 tbsp fresh chopped parsley

¾ cup corn kernels

ground black pepper

≈ Heat the vegetable broth in a pan, add the rice and onion and cook for 10 minutes.

≈ Stir in the garlic, chestnuts, celery, parsley, and corn. Season well and cook for 40 minutes over a low heat until the rice is cooked and the liquid has been absorbed.

NUTRITION FACTS	
Serving Size 1 (148g)	
Calories 155	Calories from Fat 9
	% Daily Value
Total Fat 1g	2%
Saturated Fat 0g	1%
Monounsaturated Fat 0.4g	0%
Polyunsaturated Fat 0.4g	0%
Cholesterol 0mg	0%
Sodium 181mg	8%
Total Carbohydrate 34g	11%
Dietary Fiber 2g	8%
Sugars 5g	0%
Protein 4g	0%

Percent daily values are based on a 2000 calorie diet

VEGETABLE GRATINÉE

SERVES 4

This colorful combination of baked vegetables is topped with bread crumbs, cilantro, and cheese for added flavor and texture. It would make a perfect side dish or a light meal.

2 leeks, cut into strips lengthwise

2 carrots, cut into sticks

½ cup snow peas

1 cup baby corn, halved

2 garlic cloves, minced

1 tbsp clear honey

½ tsp ground ginger

¼ tsp grated nutmeg

⅔ cup apple juice

⅔ cup vegetable broth

1 cup fresh white bread crumbs

2 tbsp fresh chopped cilantro

¼ cup low-fat cheese, shredded

≈ Place the vegetables in a large pan of boiling water and cook for 10 minutes. Drain well and place in a shallow oven-proof dish.

≈ Mix together the garlic, honey, ginger, nutmeg, apple juice, and broth, and pour over the vegetables.

≈ Mix together the bread crumbs and cilantro. Sprinkle over the vegetables to cover. Top with the cheese. Bake in the oven at 400°F for 45 minutes or until golden brown. Serve.

NUTRITION FACTS	
Serving Size 1 (243g)	
Calories 164	Calories from Fat 18
	% Daily Value
Total Fat 2g	3%
Saturated Fat 0g	2%
Monounsaturated Fat 0.4g	0%
Polyunsaturated Fat 0.4g	0%
Cholesterol 2mg	1%
Sodium 363mg	15%
Total Carbohydrate 34g	11%
Dietary Fiber 3g	12%
Sugars 13g	0%
Protein 6g	0%

Percent daily values are based on a 2000 calorie diet

Vegetable Gratinée ▶

SPICED EGGPLANT

SERVES 4

An Indian eggplant dish which is perfect with curry or a plain vegetable casserole. Spicy in itself, it is also delicious cold as an appetizer.

1 lb eggplant

6 oz potatoes

4 tbsp vegetable broth

½ onion, sliced

1 small red bell pepper, seeded and diced

¼ tsp ground coriander

¼ tsp ground cumin

1 tsp fresh ginger, shredded

½ tsp curry powder

3 garlic cloves, minced

1 tsp chili powder

dash of ground turmeric

dash of sugar

1 green chile, diced

1 tbsp fresh chopped cilantro

NUTRITION FACTS	
Serving Size 1 (206g)	
Calories 110	Calories from Fat 9
	% Daily Value
Total Fat 1g	1%
Saturated Fat 0g	0%
Monounsaturated Fat 0.0g	0%
Polyunsaturated Fat 0.1g	0%
Cholesterol 0mg	0%
Sodium 78mg	3%
Total Carbohydrate 25g	8%
Dietary Fiber 5g	20%
Sugars 3g	0%
Protein 3g	0%

Percent daily values are based on a 2000 calorie diet

≈ Dice the eggplant into small cubes. Cut the potatoes into 1-inch chunks.
≈ Heat the broth in a pan, add the onion and cook for 2–3 minutes. Stir in the red pepper, ground coriander, cumin, ginger, curry powder, garlic, chili powder, and turmeric, and cook for 2–3 minutes.

≈ Add the eggplant, sugar, green chile, and ⅔ cup water, cover and simmer for 15 minutes. Add the potato, re-cover and cook for 10 minutes. Stir in the fresh cilantro and serve.

STEAMED HONEY-GLAZED PARSNIPS

SERVES 4

Traditionally parsnips are roasted or baked, but they steam equally well and in far less time.

≈ Cook the parsnips in boiling water for 5 minutes. Drain well and place in a steamer lined with foil.
≈ Mix together the honey, ginger, cumin seeds, vegetable broth, and cilantro. Pour over the parsnips and season. Cover and steam for 20 minutes or until cooked through. Serve immediately with the cooking liquid.

8 baby parsnips
2 tbsp honey
½ tsp ground ginger
½ tsp cumin seeds
8 tbsp vegetable broth
1 tbsp fresh chopped cilantro
ground black pepper

NUTRITION FACTS	
Serving Size 1 (100g)	
Calories 90	Calories from Fat 0
	% Daily Value
Total Fat 0g	1%
Saturated Fat 0g	0%
Monounsaturated Fat 0.1g	0%
Polyunsaturated Fat 0.0g	0%
Cholesterol 0mg	0%
Sodium 80mg	3%
Total Carbohydrate 22g	7%
Dietary Fiber 3g	13%
Sugars 9g	0%
Protein 2g	0%

Percent daily values are based on a 2000 calorie diet

MIXED VEGETABLE DUMPLINGS

MAKES 24

These are like Chinese dumplings or Dim Sum. A water and flour dough encases delicately chopped vegetables. Quickly steamed they are perfect with a Chinese main course.

≈ Mix all the filling ingredients together in a bowl.
≈ Place 2½ cups of the flour for the dough in a bowl. Stir in ½ cup boiling water, ¼ cup cold water and the oil. Bring the mixture together to form a dough. Sprinkle the remaining flour on a work surface and knead the dough until smooth. Roll the dough into a long sausage shape and cut into 24 equal pieces. Roll each piece into a 2-inch round.

≈ Divide the filling into 24 and spoon into the center of each round. Bring the edges of the dough together in the center and pinch together to seal as a parcel.
≈ Line a steamer with a damp cloth, place one-quarter of the dumplings in the steamer and steam for 5 minutes. Repeat with the remaining dumplings and serve.

For the filling
1 small carrot, chopped fine
1 celery stalk, chopped
1 green onion, chopped
1 small zucchini, chopped fine
2 garlic cloves, minced
½ tbsp soy sauce
dash of sugar
1 tsp dry sherry
1 tbsp cornstarch

For the dough
3 cups all-purpose flour
1 tbsp polyunsaturated oil

NUTRITION FACTS	
Serving Size 1 (29g)	
Calories 68	Calories from Fat 9
	% Daily Value
Total Fat 1g	1%
Saturated Fat 0g	0%
Monounsaturated Fat 0.0g	0%
Polyunsaturated Fat 0.4g	0%
Cholesterol 0mg	0%
Sodium 25mg	1%
Total Carbohydrate 13g	4%
Dietary Fiber 1g	3%
Sugars 1g	0%
Protein 2g	0%

Percent daily values are based on a 2000 calorie diet

SWEET RED CABBAGE

SERVES 4

Colorful and with a sweet and sour flavor, it may also be served cold.

1¼ cups vegetable broth

1½ lb red cabbage, cored and shredded

1 onion, sliced

1 tbsp granulated brown sugar

1 tsp ground allspice

8 oz green apples, cored and sliced

1 tsp fennel seeds

2 tbsp cider vinegar

1 tbsp cornstarch

1 tbsp fresh chopped parsley

≈ Place half of the broth in a large saucepan. Add the cabbage and onion and cook over a high heat for 5 minutes. ≈ Add the sugar, allspice, apples, fennel seeds, vinegar, and remaining broth. Blend the cornstarch with 2 tablespoons of cold water to form a paste. Stir into the pan and bring to a boil, stirring until thickened and clear.

≈ Reduce the heat and cook for a further 15 minutes until the cabbage is cooked. Sprinkle with the parsley and serve.

NUTRITION FACTS	
Serving Size 1 (328g)	
Calories 106	Calories from Fat 9
	% Daily Value
Total Fat 1g	1%
Saturated Fat 0g	1%
Monounsaturated Fat 0.0g	0%
Polyunsaturated Fat 0.3g	0%
Cholesterol 0mg	0%
Sodium 178mg	7%
Total Carbohydrate 24g	8%
Dietary Fiber 3g	13%
Sugars 11g	0%
Protein 3g	0%

Percent daily values are based on a 2000 calorie diet

CARAMELIZED BAKED ONIONS

SERVES 4

These baked onions have a slightly "burnt" taste which complements the sweetness of the onion. Serve with a simple main dish.

4 large onions

2 tsp polyunsaturated margarine

5 tbsp granulated brown sugar

≈ Cut the onions into quarters and then into four again. Cook in boiling water for 10 minutes. Drain well.

≈ Place the margarine and sugar in a pan and heat gently until melted. Place the onions in a roasting pan and pour over the margarine and sugar. Cook in the oven at 375°F for 10 minutes until browned. Serve immediately.

NUTRITION FACTS	
Serving Size 1 (10g)	
Calories 31	Calories from Fat 9
	% Daily Value
Total Fat 1g	1%
Saturated Fat 0g	1%
Monounsaturated Fat 0.4g	0%
Polyunsaturated Fat 0.3g	0%
Cholesterol 0mg	0%
Sodium 3mg	0%
Total Carbohydrate 6g	2%
Dietary Fiber 0g	0%
Sugars 0g	0%
Protein 0g	0%

Percent daily values are based on a 2000 calorie diet

Sweet Red Cabbage ▶

HOT SPICY LENTILS

SERVES 4

An example of using lentils in place of meat, this recipe can be eaten as a side dish or as a vegetarian meal.

≈ Wash the lentils in 2–3 changes of water. Drain and reserve. Heat the oil in a pan, add the onion, garlic, and spices and cook for 5 minutes. Stir in the lentils and cook for a further 3–4 minutes.

≈ Add the chile and broth and bring to a boil. Reduce the heat and simmer gently for 35 minutes until the lentils are soft. Stir in the lime juice and rind. Season well and serve.

¾ cup red lentils

4 tsp polyunsaturated oil

1 red onion, chopped

2 garlic cloves, minced

¼ tsp ground cumin

¼ tsp ground coriander

1 red chile, chopped

3¾ cups vegetable broth

juice and grated rind of 1 lime

ground black pepper

NUTRITION FACTS

Serving Size 1 (237g)

Calories 186	Calories from Fat 45

	% Daily Value
Total Fat 5g	8%
Saturated Fat 0g	2%
Monounsaturated Fat 0.6g	0%
Polyunsaturated Fat 3.5g	0%
Cholesterol 0mg	0%
Sodium 59mg	2%
Total Carbohydrate 23g	8%
Dietary Fiber 12g	46%
Sugars 0g	0%
Protein 14g	0%

Percent daily values are based on a 2000 calorie diet

THREE-MUSHROOM FRY

SERVES 4

This really is a simple yet delicious dish. Three varieties of mushroom are cooked in garlic and soy sauce.

≈ Peel the open cap mushrooms and thinly slice. Place all the mushrooms in a skillet with the broth, garlic, soy sauce, and half of the herbs. Season well with black pepper. Cook, stirring, for 3–4 minutes. Sprinkle in the remaining herbs and serve immediately.

1 cup open cap mushrooms

1 cup oyster mushrooms

1 cup shiitake mushrooms

4 tbsp vegetable broth

2 garlic cloves, minced

1 tbsp soy sauce

2 tbsp fresh chopped parsley or thyme

ground black pepper

NUTRITION FACTS

Serving Size 1 (129g)

Calories 71	Calories from Fat 0

	% Daily Value
Total Fat 0g	1%
Saturated Fat 0g	1%
Monounsaturated Fat 0.1g	0%
Polyunsaturated Fat 0.0g	0%
Cholesterol 0mg	0%
Sodium 289mg	12%
Total Carbohydrate 18g	6%
Dietary Fiber 3g	12%
Sugars 0g	0%
Protein 2g	0%

Percent daily values are based on a 2000 calorie diet

Three-Mushroom Fry ▶

RATATOUILLE

SERVES 4

A medley of vegetables cooked in a tomato and herb sauce. This is a strongly flavored dish to be served with a plainer recipe or used to top a jacket potato.

1 onion, halved and sliced

2 garlic cloves, minced

⅔ cup vegetable broth

1 large eggplant, sliced

6 oz zucchini, sliced

1 yellow bell pepper, seeded and
    sliced

2 tbsp tomato paste

14 oz can chopped tomatoes

6 oz canned artichoke hearts,
    drained

2 tbsp fresh chopped oregano

ground black pepper

NUTRITION FACTS	
Serving Size 1 (351g)	
Calories 83	Calories from Fat 9
	% Daily Value
Total Fat 1g	1%
Saturated Fat 0g	0%
Monounsaturated Fat 0.0g	0%
Polyunsaturated Fat 0.1g	0%
Cholesterol 0mg	0%
Sodium 228mg	10%
Total Carbohydrate 17g	6%
Dietary Fiber 3g	12%
Sugars 2g	0%
Protein 4g	0%

Percent daily values are based on a 2000 calorie diet

≈ Place the onion, garlic, and broth in a skillet and cook for 5 minutes until the onion softens. Add the eggplant, zucchini, and yellow pepper and cook for a further 5 minutes.

≈ Stir in the tomato paste, chopped tomatoes, and 1 tablespoon of the oregano. Season well. Bring to a boil, cover and reduce the heat. Cook for 1 hour, stirring occasionally. Sprinkle with the remaining oregano and serve.

HERB GNOCCHI

SERVES 4

An Italian favorite, gnocchi can be made from potato, flour, or a mixture of the two. They may be boiled, baked, or broiled for a traditional accompaniment.

≈ Place the milk and broth in a saucepan and bring to a boil. Add to the cooked potato, with the coriander, egg white, margarine, and ½ cup of the cheese, stirring well.

≈ Spread the mixture into a shallow, lightly greased ovenproof dish and allow to cool. Sprinkle on the remaining cheese and broil for 5 minutes. Cut into squares and serve.

¼ cup skim milk

¼ cup vegetable broth

1½ lb cooked potato, mashed

ground black pepper

¼ tsp ground coriander

1 egg white, beaten

2 tbsp polyunsaturated margarine

¾ cup low-fat cheese, shredded

NUTRITION FACTS	
Serving Size 1 (144g)	
Calories 165	Calories from Fat 36
	% Daily Value
Total Fat 4g	6%
Saturated Fat 1g	4%
Monounsaturated Fat 1.7g	0%
Polyunsaturated Fat 1.2g	0%
Cholesterol 0mg	0%
Sodium 109mg	5%
Total Carbohydrate 30g	10%
Dietary Fiber 3g	11%
Sugars 2g	0%
Protein 4g	0%

Percent daily values are based on a 2000 calorie diet

QUICK SPICED RICE

SERVES 4

Unlike a risotto, the rice in this recipe is cooked separately and stirred into the vegetables at the end of cooking. This halves the cooking time to give a speedy vegetable meal or side dish.

≈ Place the broth in a skillet, add the beans, corn, jalapeño chile, tomatoes, celery, garlic, and onion. Cook for 7 minutes, stirring. Add the asparagus, cayenne pepper, and chili powder and cook for a further 3 minutes.

≈ Meanwhile, cook the rice in boiling water and drain well. Stir the rice into the pan with the vegetables. Sprinkle with parsley and serve.

1¼ cups vegetable broth

8 oz fine beans, trimmed

¾ cup corn kernels

1 pickled jalapeño chile, sliced

2 oz sundried tomatoes, soaked in water overnight and sliced

2 celery stalks, sliced

3 garlic cloves, minced

1 red onion, diced

4 asparagus spears, sliced

¼ tsp cayenne pepper

¼ tsp chili powder

generous cup long-grain brown rice

1 tbsp fresh chopped parsley

NUTRITION FACTS	
Serving Size 1 (274g)	
Calories 157	Calories from Fat 18
	% Daily Value
Total Fat 2g	3%
Saturated Fat 0g	2%
Monounsaturated Fat 0.4g	0%
Polyunsaturated Fat 0.6g	0%
Cholesterol 0mg	0%
Sodium 608mg	25%
Total Carbohydrate 32g	11%
Dietary Fiber 6g	23%
Sugars 3g	0%
Protein 7g	0%

Percent daily values are based on a 2000 calorie diet

DELICATE DESSERTS

Honeyed Oranges

Strawberry Fool

Apricot Sherbet

Melon Ice

Frudités

Blueberry Crush

Apple Crumb Pie

Banana Ice Cream

Vanilla Mousse

Blueberry Cheesecake

Crème Caramel

Plum and Ginger Brûlée

Cappuccino Sponges

Cinnamon Toasts

Baked Apples

Poached Pears

HONEYED ORANGES

SERVES 4

Oranges and ginger make a great combination. Ground ginger has been added to this recipe with a dash of orange liqueur for extra flavor.

≈ Place the honey, cinnamon, ginger, and mint in a pan with ⅔ cup water. Heat gently to melt the honey. Bring to a boil and boil for 3 minutes to reduce by half. Remove the mint from the pan and discard. Stir in the Grand Marnier.

≈ Meanwhile, peel the oranges, remove the pith and slice thinly. Place the orange slices in a serving bowl, pour over the syrup and chill for 1 hour before serving.

4 tbsp honey

½ tsp ground cinnamon

¼ tsp ground ginger

2 mint sprigs

2 tsp Grand Marnier

4 oranges

NUTRITION FACTS

Serving Size 1 (253g)

Calories 141	Calories from Fat 0

	% Daily Value
Total Fat 0g	1%
Saturated Fat 0g	0%
Monounsaturated Fat 0.0g	0%
Polyunsaturated Fat 0.0g	0%
Cholesterol 0mg	0%
Sodium 4mg	0%
Total Carbohydrate 34g	11%
Dietary Fiber 10g	40%
Sugars 37g	0%
Protein 2g	0%

Percent daily values are based on a 2000 calorie diet

STRAWBERRY FOOL

SERVES 4

This dish is simple to prepare, but should be made in advance of a meal as it requires chilling for 1 hour before serving.

≈ Place the chopped strawberries in a food processor with the powdered sugar. Blend for 30 seconds until smooth.

≈ Place the yogurt in a bowl and stir in the strawberry mixture. Whisk the egg whites until peaks form and fold in gently. Spoon into serving glasses and chill for 1 hour. Decorate and serve.

10 oz strawberries, hulled and
   chopped

½ cup powdered sugar

1¼ cups low-fat plain yogurt

2 egg whites

strawberry slices and mint sprigs to
   decorate

NUTRITION FACTS

Serving Size 1 (181g)

Calories 136	Calories from Fat 9

	% Daily Value
Total Fat 1g	2%
Saturated Fat 1g	4%
Monounsaturated Fat 0.3g	0%
Polyunsaturated Fat 0.1g	0%
Cholesterol 4mg	1%
Sodium 79mg	3%
Total Carbohydrate 25g	8%
Dietary Fiber 2g	7%
Sugars 8g	0%
Protein 6g	0%

Percent daily values are based on a 2000 calorie diet

Honeyed Oranges ▶

¾ cup granulated sugar

juice of ½ orange

1 lb apricots, pitted and chopped

1 egg white

2 tbsp fine granulated sugar

apricot slices, mint sprigs, and
    orange rind to decorate

NUTRITION FACTS	
Serving Size 1 (210g)	
Calories 247	Calories from Fat 9
	% Daily Value
Total Fat 1g	1%
Saturated Fat 0g	0%
Monounsaturated Fat 0.2g	0%
Polyunsaturated Fat 0.1g	0%
Cholesterol 0mg	0%
Sodium 16mg	1%
Total Carbohydrate 61g	20%
Dietary Fiber 3g	13%
Sugars 56g	0%
Protein 3g	0%

Percent daily values are based on a 2000 calorie diet

APRICOT SHERBET

SERVES 4

*Sherbets are always refreshing and this is no exception. Traditionally they are
served part way through a meal to clear the palate, but are equally welcome
at the end.*

≈ Set the freezer to rapid freeze. Place
the sugar and orange juice in a pan with
⅔ cup water. Cook over gentle heat to
dissolve. Add a further 1¼ cups water to
the pan.

≈ Place the apricots in a food processor
and purée for 30 seconds until smooth.
Stir the apricot purée into the sugar
syrup, place in a freezerproof container
and freeze for 1 hour until half frozen.
Whisk the egg white in a clean bowl
until peaking and whisk in the sugar.

≈ Turn the half frozen fruit mixture
into a bowl and whisk until smooth.
Fold in the egg white and return to a
freezerproof container. Freeze for
45 minutes.

≈ Turn the mixture out into a bowl,
whisk again and return to a clean
freezerproof container. Freeze for a
further 2 hours until solid. Place the
sherbet in the refrigerator 10 minutes
before serving. Scoop into serving
dishes, decorate and serve.

½ cup granulated sugar

3 mint sprigs

1 lb melon, such as cantaloupe,
    galia, or watermelon, seeded
    and diced

mint to decorate

NUTRITION FACTS	
Serving Size 1 (149g)	
Calories 137	Calories from Fat 0
	% Daily Value
Total Fat 0g	0%
Saturated Fat 0g	0%
Monounsaturated Fat 0.0g	0%
Polyunsaturated Fat 0.0g	0%
Cholesterol 0mg	0%
Sodium 25mg	1%
Total Carbohydrate 34g	12%
Dietary Fiber 1g	5%
Sugars 24g	0%
Protein 1g	0%

Percent daily values are based on a 2000 calorie diet

MELON ICE

SERVES 4

*Any melon is suitable for this recipe. Incredibly colorful and refreshing, it is the
perfect light end to any meal.*

≈ Set the freezer to rapid freeze. Place
the granulated sugar in a pan with ½ cup
water. Add the mint and cook over a
gentle heat until the sugar dissolves.
Remove the pan from the heat and strain
the syrup. Discard the mint sprigs. Stir
in 1¼ cups of cold water.

≈ Place the melon in a food processor
and purée for 30 seconds until smooth.
Stir into the syrup. Mix well and cool.
Place the mixture in a freezerproof
container and freeze for 1 hour.

≈ Remove from the freezer and pour the
melon mixture into a bowl and whisk
until smooth. Return to a clean freezerproof container and freeze for a further
30 minutes. Repeat the whisking process
every 30 minutes for 2½ hours. Scoop
into dishes, decorate with mint, and
serve immediately.

Melon Ice ▶

FRUDITÉS

SERVES 4

A sweet variation of "crudités," this recipe is simple and easy to eat.
An informal dessert to be shared with friends.

scant cup strawberries, halved

1 green eating apple, cored and
   sliced

2 bananas, cut into 1 inch chunks

1 Chinese gooseberry, cut into eight

2 tsp lemon juice

fresh mint to decorate

For the yogurt dip

1 cup low-fat plain yogurt

1 tbsp granulated brown sugar

dash of ground cinnamon

1 small papaya, seeded and diced

mint and cinnamon to decorate

NUTRITION FACTS	
Serving Size 1 (268g)	
Calories 162	Calories from Fat 18
	% Daily Value
Total Fat 2g	3%
Saturated Fat 1g	4%
Monounsaturated Fat 0.3g	0%
Polyunsaturated Fat 0.3g	0%
Cholesterol 3mg	1%
Sodium 44mg	2%
Total Carbohydrate 35g	12%
Dietary Fiber 5g	21%
Sugars 25g	0%
Protein 4g	0%

Percent daily values are based on a 2000 calorie diet

≈ Prepare all the fruits. Sprinkle the apple and banana with the lemon juice.

≈ Place the yogurt dip ingredients in a food processor and blend for 30 seconds until smooth. Spoon into a serving bowl. Place the dip on a large serving plate, sprinkle with cinnamon, and arrange the fruit around. Serve with sprigs of mint.

100

BLUEBERRY CRUSH

SERVES 4

This is really quick to prepare, but requires freezing. Perfect to serve at a dinner party if you make it in advance.

≈ Place the meringues in a bowl. Add the blueberries and yogurt and mix well. Line a 3¾ cup pudding bowl with plastic wrap and spoon in the mixture, pressing down well. Place in the freezer for 2 hours or until firm.
≈ Meanwhile for the sauce, place the blueberries, sugar, and cranberry juice in a food processor. Blend for 30 seconds until smooth. Press through a sieve and chill until required.

≈ Dip the pudding bowl into hot water for 4 seconds. Invert the bowl onto a serving plate and unmold the pudding. Serve with the blueberry sauce.

5 oz cooked meringue, broken into pieces
1 cup blueberries
1¼ cups low-fat plain yogurt

For the sauce

1 cup blueberries
2 tbsp powdered sugar
4 tbsp cranberry juice

NUTRITION FACTS	
Serving Size 1 (198g)	
Calories 216	Calories from Fat 9
	% Daily Value
Total Fat 1g	2%
Saturated Fat 1g	4%
Monounsaturated Fat 0.3g	0%
Polyunsaturated Fat 0.0g	0%
Cholesterol 4mg	1%
Sodium 97mg	4%
Total Carbohydrate 45g	15%
Dietary Fiber 2g	8%
Sugars 11g	0%
Protein 7g	0%

Percent daily values are based on a 2000 calorie diet

APPLE CRUMB PIE

SERVES 8–12

A deep dish apple pie using filo or strudel pastry as the crust. Topped with a crumble mixture it is delicious served with plain yogurt.

≈ Lay a sheet of filo pastry in the base of a pie dish and up the sides. Brush lightly with melted margarine and continue layering pastry to cover the sides of the pie dish. Brush each sheet with margarine. Cook the pastry in the oven at 400°F for 10 minutes.

≈ Meanwhile, place the apples, sugar, raisins, and nutmeg in a pan. Cover and cook for 10 minutes or until the apples have softened. Mix together the topping ingredients.
≈ Spoon the apple filling into the pastry lined dish. Sprinkle on the topping, return to the oven and cook for 40 minutes until golden.

5 oz filo pastry
1½ tbsp polyunsaturated margarine, melted
2 lb cooking apples, peeled and sliced
2 tbsp granulated brown sugar
2 tbsp raisins
dash of grated nutmeg

For the topping

6 tbsp all-purpose flour
½ cup oatmeal
¼ cup granulated brown sugar
2 tbsp polyunsaturated margarine

NUTRITION FACTS	
Serving Size 1 (161g)	
Calories 247	Calories from Fat 63
	% Daily Value
Total Fat 7g	11%
Saturated Fat 1g	6%
Monounsaturated Fat 2.5g	0%
Polyunsaturated Fat 2.3g	0%
Cholesterol 0mg	0%
Sodium 149mg	6%
Total Carbohydrate 45g	15%
Dietary Fiber 4g	16%
Sugars 11g	0%
Protein 3g	0%

Percent daily values are based on a 2000 calorie diet

BANANA ICE CREAM

SERVES 4

½ lb bananas, chopped and frozen

1 tbsp lemon juice

6 tbsp powdered sugar

⅔ cup low-fat plain yogurt

grated rind of 1 lemon

small meringues to serve (optional)

This is really a cheat ice cream. Made with frozen bananas and plain yogurt, the freezing time of the completed recipe is greatly reduced.

≈ Set the freezer to rapid freeze. Place the frozen bananas in a food processor with the lemon juice, powdered sugar, and yogurt. Process for 1 minute or until smooth. Stir in the lemon rind.

≈ Place the mixture in a freezerproof container, cover and freeze for 2 hours or until set. Scoop into dishes and serve with small meringues.

NUTRITION FACTS	
Serving Size 1 (115g)	
Calories 114	Calories from Fat 9
	% Daily Value
Total Fat 1g	1%
Saturated Fat 0g	2%
Monounsaturated Fat 0.2g	0%
Polyunsaturated Fat 0.0g	0%
Cholesterol 2mg	1%
Sodium 27mg	1%
Total Carbohydrate 32g	11%
Dietary Fiber 1g	6%
Sugars 20g	0%
Protein 3g	0%

Percent daily values are based on a 2000 calorie diet

VANILLA MOUSSE

SERVES 4

This light and fluffy mousse tastes as good as it looks. Sliced and served with the raspberry sauce it is a dieter's dream.

For the mousse

1¼ cups low-fat plain yogurt

⅔ cup skim milk cheese or low-fat
   cream cheese

1 tsp vanilla extract

4 tbsp vanilla sugar

1 tbsp brandy or sherry

2 tsp vegetarian gelatin

2 large egg whites

For the sauce

1¾ cups raspberries

juice of 1 orange

¼ cup powdered sugar, sieved

≈ Place the yogurt, cheese, vanilla extract, sugar, and alcohol in a food processor, blend for 30 seconds until smooth. Pour into a mixing bowl.

≈ Sprinkle the gelatin onto 4 tablespoons of cold water. Stir until dissolved and heat to boiling point. Boil for 2 minutes. Cool. Stir into the yogurt mixture. Whisk the egg whites until peaking and fold into the mousse.

≈ Line a 3¾ cup loaf pan with plastic wrap. Pour the mousse into the prepared pan and chill for 2 hours until set.

≈ Meanwhile, place the sauce ingredients in a food processor and blend until smooth. Press through a sieve to discard the seeds. Unmold the mousse onto a plate, remove the plastic wrap, slice and serve with the sauce.

NUTRITION FACTS	
Serving Size 1 (248g)	
Calories 373	Calories from Fat 9
	% Daily Value
Total Fat 1g	2%
Saturated Fat 1g	4%
Monounsaturated Fat 0.3g	0%
Polyunsaturated Fat 0.2g	0%
Cholesterol 4mg	1%
Sodium 82mg	3%
Total Carbohydrate 51g	17%
Dietary Fiber 3g	11%
Sugars 22g	0%
Protein 10g	0%

Percent daily values are based on a 2000 calorie diet

Vanilla Mousse ▶

BLUEBERRY CHEESECAKE

SERVES 6

A cheesecake with a delicious granola and dried fig base, in place of the usual cookies and butter, which gives a rich and crunchy base to the soft filling.

For the base

1 cup natural granola

5 oz dried figs

For the filling

1 tsp vegetarian gelatin

½ cup skim evaporated milk

1 egg

6 tbsp fine granulated sugar

1 lb low-fat cottage cheese

½ cup blueberries

For the topping

2 cups blueberries

2 nectarines, pitted and sliced

2 tbsp honey

≈ Place the granola and dried figs in a food processor and blend together for 30 seconds. Press into the base of a base lined 8-inch springclip pan and chill while preparing the filling.

≈ Sprinkle the gelatin onto 4 tablespoons of cold water. Stir until dissolved and heat to boiling point. Boil for 2 minutes. Cool. Place the milk, egg, sugar, and cheese in a food processor and blend until smooth. Stir in the blueberries. Place in a mixing bowl and gradually stir in the dissolved gelatin. Pour the mixture onto the base and chill for 2 hours until set.

≈ Remove the cheesecake from the pan and arrange the fruit for the topping in alternate rings on top. Drizzle the honey over the fruit and serve.

NUTRITION FACTS	
Serving Size 1 (238g)	
Calories 215	Calories from Fat 18
	% Daily Value
Total Fat 2g	3%
Saturated Fat 1g	4%
Monounsaturated Fat 0.6g	0%
Polyunsaturated Fat 0.2g	0%
Cholesterol 39mg	13%
Sodium 333mg	14%
Total Carbohydrate 40g	13%
Dietary Fiber 3g	13%
Sugars 44g	0%
Protein 13g	0%

Percent daily values are based on a 2000 calorie diet

CRÈME CARAMEL

MAKES 4

Although low in fat, this recipe uses two whole eggs and should therefore follow a main course which does not use eggs to balance the fat content of the meal.

½ cup plus 2 tsp fine granulated
   sugar

2 eggs, beaten

1¼ cups skim milk

½ tsp vanilla extract

dash of ground cinnamon

≈ Dissolve the ½ cup sugar in a pan with ⅔ cup cold water. Bring to a boil and boil rapidly until the mixture begins to turn golden brown. Pour into the base of 4 × ⅔ cup ramekin dishes.

≈ Whisk the remaining sugar with the eggs in a bowl. Heat the milk with the vanilla and cinnamon until just boiling and gradually whisk into the egg mixture.

≈ Pour into the ramekins and place in a shallow roasting pan with enough hot water to reach halfway up the sides. Cover and cook in the oven at 350°F for 50 minutes until set. Remove from the pan, slightly cool and chill in the refrigerator for 1 hour. Unmold onto individual plates and serve immediately.

Blueberry Cheesecake ▶

NUTRITION FACTS	
Serving Size 1 (130g)	
Calories 171	Calories from Fat 18
	% Daily Value
Total Fat 2g	4%
Saturated Fat 1g	4%
Monounsaturated Fat 1.0g	0%
Polyunsaturated Fat 0.3g	0%
Cholesterol 106mg	35%
Sodium 71mg	3%
Total Carbohydrate 32g	10%
Dietary Fiber 0g	0%
Sugars 30g	0%
Protein 6g	0%

Percent daily values are based on a 2000 calorie diet

PLUM AND GINGER BRÛLÉE

SERVES 4

Plums and ginger are a great combination in this easy brûlée recipe, the ginger adding just enough spice to complement the plums.

4 plums, pitted and chopped

scant 1 cup half-fat cream substitute

scant 1 cup low-fat plain yogurt

½ tsp ground ginger

4 tbsp granulated brown sugar

≈ Spoon the plums into the base of 4 × ⅔ cup ramekin dishes. Lightly whip the cream substitute and fold in the yogurt and ground ginger. Spoon onto the fruit and chill for 2 hours.

≈ Sprinkle the brown sugar on top of the yogurt mixture and broil for 5 minutes or until the sugar has dissolved. Chill for 20 minutes before serving.

NUTRITION FACTS	
Serving Size 1 (479g)	
Calories 344	Calories from Fat 27
	% Daily Value
Total Fat 3g	4%
Saturated Fat 1g	4%
Monounsaturated Fat 1.4g	0%
Polyunsaturated Fat 0.4g	0%
Cholesterol 4mg	1%
Sodium 86mg	4%
Total Carbohydrate 74g	25%
Dietary Fiber 4g	14%
Sugars 46g	0%
Protein 8g	0%

Percent daily values are based on a 2000 calorie diet

CAPPUCCINO SPONGES

SERVES 4

These individual sponge puddings are delicious served with the low-fat coffee sauce. Ideal for dinner parties, they look more delicate and attractive than one large pudding.

2 tbsp polyunsaturated margarine

2 tbsp granulated brown sugar

2 egg whites

½ cup all-purpose flour

¾ tsp baking powder

6 tbsp skim milk

1 tsp coffee extract

½ tsp unsweetened cocoa powder

For the coffee sauce

1¼ cups skim milk

1 tbsp granulated brown sugar

1 tsp coffee extract

1 tsp coffee liqueur (optional)

2 tbsp cornstarch

≈ Use nonstick spray to lightly grease 4 × ⅔ cup individual pudding molds. Cream the margarine and the sugar together in a bowl and add the egg whites. Sieve the flour and baking powder together and fold into the creamed mixture with a metal spoon. Gradually stir in the milk, coffee extract, and cocoa.

≈ Spoon equal amounts of the mixture into the molds. Cover with pleated wax paper, then foil, and tie securely with string. Place in a steamer or pan with sufficient boiling water to reach halfway up the sides of the molds. Cover and cook for 30 minutes or until cooked through.

≈ Meanwhile, place the milk, sugar, coffee extract, and coffee liqueur in a pan to make the sauce. Blend the cornstarch with 4 tablespoons of cold water and stir into the pan. Bring to a boil, stirring until thickened. Reduce the heat and cook for a further 2–3 minutes.

≈ Carefully remove the cooked puddings from the steamer. Remove the paper and foil and unmold onto individual plates. Spoon the sauce around and serve.

NUTRITION FACTS	
Serving Size 1 (154g)	
Calories 199	Calories from Fat 54
	% Daily Value
Total Fat 6g	9%
Saturated Fat 1g	6%
Monounsaturated Fat 2.6g	0%
Polyunsaturated Fat 1.9g	0%
Cholesterol 2mg	1%
Sodium 241mg	10%
Total Carbohydrate 29g	10%
Dietary Fiber 1g	2%
Sugars 12g	0%
Protein 7g	0%

Percent daily values are based on a 2000 calorie diet

Plum and Ginger Brûlée ▶

CINNAMON TOASTS

SERVES 4

This recipe is based on the classic breakfast dish. Here cinnamon is added to the milk and egg mixture to give a warm, spicy flavor to the recipe.

4 thick slices white bread, crusts
    removed and halved diagonally

2/3 cup skim milk

1 tsp ground cinnamon

1 egg, beaten

2 oranges, peeled, halved and sliced

2 Chinese gooseberries, peeled,
    halved and thinly sliced

4 tsp granulated brown sugar

For the yogurt sauce

⅔ cup low-fat plain yogurt

2 tsp honey

dash of ground cinnamon

cinnamon to sprinkle

NUTRITION FACTS	
Serving Size 1 (228g)	
Calories 198	Calories from Fat 27
	% Daily Value
Total Fat 3g	5%
Saturated Fat 1g	6%
Monounsaturated Fat 1.1g	0%
Polyunsaturated Fat 0.5g	0%
Cholesterol 56mg	18%
Sodium 195mg	8%
Total Carbohydrate 36g	12%
Dietary Fiber 4g	17%
Sugars 20g	0%
Protein 8g	0%

Percent daily values are based on a 2000 calorie diet

≈ Arrange the bread in a shallow dish. Mix together the milk, cinnamon, and egg and pour over the bread. Let sit for 30 minutes.

≈ Remove the bread from the dish and cook one side under the broiler for 4–5 minutes. Turn the bread over and broil for 2 minutes.

≈ Arrange the fruit in alternate layers on top of the bread and sprinkle each with 1 teaspoon of sugar. Broil for 3 minutes until the sugar begins to dissolve.

≈ Mix together the yogurt sauce ingredients, sprinkle with cinnamon, and serve with the hot cinnamon toasts.

BAKED APPLES

SERVES 4

Usually filled with a suet-based mincemeat mixture, baked apples are a wonderful winter dessert. In this recipe, dried fruits and sugar have been used as a low-fat alternative.

≈ Wash the apples, dry, and remove the cores. Mix together the raisins, apricots, mixed peel, dates, margarine, sugar, and lemon rind. Spoon into the hollowed centers of the apples. Score the skin around the apple, approximately 1 inch from the top.

≈ Stand the apples in an ovenproof dish and pour a little water around them. Bake in the oven at 350°F for 45 minutes or until cooked.

≈ Meanwhile, mix together the yogurt, honey, and lemon rind. Remove the apples from the dish and serve with the yogurt.

4 large cooking apples

3 tbsp raisins

2 tbsp dried apricots, chopped fine

3 tbsp chopped mixed candied peel

¼ cup pitted dried dates, chopped fine

1 tbsp polyunsaturated margarine

2 tbsp granulated brown sugar

grated rind of 1 lemon

For the yogurt sauce

⅔ cup low-fat plain yogurt

2 tsp honey

grated rind of ½ lemon

NUTRITION FACTS	
Serving Size 1 (219g)	
Calories 233	Calories from Fat 36
	% Daily Value
Total Fat 4g	6%
Saturated Fat 1g	5%
Monounsaturated Fat 1.4g	0%
Polyunsaturated Fat 1.1g	0%
Cholesterol 2mg	1%
Sodium 64mg	3%
Total Carbohydrate 50g	17%
Dietary Fiber 5g	18%
Sugars 43g	0%
Protein 3g	0%

Percent daily values are based on a 2000 calorie diet

POACHED PEARS

SERVES 4

These whole pears are cooked in alcohol and sugar to give them a delicious flavor and color. Serve with low-fat plain yogurt if preferred.

≈ Place the pears in a pan with the vermouth, ⅔ cup water, the sugar, and cassis. Heat gently to dissolve the sugar then cover and cook for 10 minutes, basting the pears occasionally.

≈ Stir in the blueberries and cook for a further 5 minutes. Transfer to a serving dish and chill until required.

4 ripe pears, peeled

⅔ cup vermouth

2 tbsp fine granulated sugar

1 tbsp cassis

½ cup blueberries

NUTRITION FACTS	
Serving Size 1 (198g)	
Calories 148	Calories from Fat 9
	% Daily Value
Total Fat 1g	1%
Saturated Fat 0g	0%
Monounsaturated Fat 0.1g	0%
Polyunsaturated Fat 0.2g	0%
Cholesterol 0mg	0%
Sodium 1mg	0%
Total Carbohydrate 35g	12%
Dietary Fiber 4g	18%
Sugars 25g	0%
Protein 1g	0%

Percent daily values are based on a 2000 calorie diet

FAVORITE CAKES, COOKIES, AND BREADS

Apple Bran Cake

Fruit and Nut Loaf

Angel Cake

Gingerbread

Oat and Orange Cookies

Raisin and Honey Bread

Chocolate Brownies

Seed Bread

Herbed Cheese Loaf

Whole Wheat Soda Bread

Pear Upside-down Cake

Rocky Mountain Buns

Apricot Bars

Low-fat Chocolate Cake

Carrot and Prune Cake

APPLE BRAN CAKE

SERVES 12

hunks of apple add moisture to this filling cake. Decorate with apple slices just before serving or brush with a little lemon juice if wishing to store the cake.

½ cup plus 2 tbsp apple sauce

½ cup plus 2 tbsp brown sugar

3 tbsp skim milk

1½ cups all-purpose flour

1 oz all bran cereal

2 tsp baking powder

1 tsp ground cinnamon

2 tbsp honey

5 oz apples, peeled and chopped

2 egg whites

apple slices and 1 tbsp honey to
decorate

≈ Grease and base line a deep 8-inch round cake pan.

≈ Place the apple sauce in a mixing bowl with the sugar and milk. Sieve the flour into the bowl and add the bran, baking powder, cinnamon, honey, and apples. Whisk the egg whites until peaking and fold into the mixture. Spoon the mixture into the prepared pan and level the surface.

≈ Bake in the oven at 150°F for 1¼–1½ hours or until cooked through. Cool in the pan for 10 minutes, then turn onto a wire rack and cool completely. Arrange the apple slices on top and drizzle with honey.

NUTRITION FACTS

Serving Size 1 (70g)

Calories 137	Calories from Fat 0

	% Daily Value
Total Fat 0g	0%
Saturated Fat 0g	0%
Monounsaturated Fat 0.0g	0%
Polyunsaturated Fat 0.1g	0%
Cholesterol 0mg	0%
Sodium 120mg	5%
Total Carbohydrate 32g	11%
Dietary Fiber 2g	7%
Sugars 16g	0%
Protein 3g	0%

Percent daily values are based on a 2000 calorie diet

FRUIT AND NUT LOAF

SERVES 12

his is a sweet fruity bread as opposed to a "tea" loaf. If liked, spread slices of the bread with a little polyunsaturated margarine to serve.

2 cups white bread flour

½ tsp salt

1 tbsp polyunsaturated margarine

1 tbsp fine granulated sugar

⅔ cup raisins

¼ cup walnuts, chopped

2 tsp active dry yeast

5 tbsp skim milk

1 tbsp honey

≈ Sieve the flour and salt into a bowl. Rub in the margarine, then stir in the sugar, raisins, walnuts, and yeast. Place the milk in a pan with 5 tablespoons of water. Heat gently until lukewarm, but do not boil. Add the lukewarm liquid to the dry ingredients in the bowl and bring the mixture together to form a dough.

≈ Turn the dough onto a lightly floured surface and knead the dough for 5–7 minutes until smooth and elastic. Shape the dough into a round and place on a nonstick baking sheet. Make parallel diagonal slits across the top of the loaf, working from left to right. Then turn the knife and work back toward you making parallel diagonal slits to form "diamond" shapes. Cover and allow to rise in a warm place for 1 hour or until doubled in size.

≈ Bake in the oven at 425°F for 35 minutes or until cooked through. Place on a wire rack and brush with honey. Cool and serve.

Apple Bran Cake ▶

NUTRITION FACTS

Serving Size 1 (44g)

Calories 139	Calories from Fat 18

	% Daily Value
Total Fat 2g	4%
Saturated Fat 0g	2%
Monounsaturated Fat 0.7g	0%
Polyunsaturated Fat 1.1g	0%
Cholesterol 0mg	0%
Sodium 113mg	5%
Total Carbohydrate 26g	9%
Dietary Fiber 1g	5%
Sugars 8g	0%
Protein 4g	0%

Percent daily values are based on a 2000 calorie diet

ANGEL CAKE

SERVES 12

Although it sounds complicated, this recipe is very easy to make. Be sure to treat the mixture gently so as not to beat out all of the air.

≈ Line 3 × 2 lb loaf pans with baking parchment paper. Whisk the eggs and sugar in a large bowl until thick and pale and the whisk leaves a trail in the mixture when lifted. Sieve the flour into the mixture and fold in gently.
≈ Divide the mixture into three equal quantities and place in separate bowls. Add a few drops of pink coloring to one bowl and stir in gently. Add a few drops of yellow food coloring to another bowl and stir in gently.

≈ Spoon the pink mixture into one prepared pan, the yellow into another and the plain mixture into the third. Bake in the oven at 400°F for 10 minutes until the mixture springs back when gently pressed. Turn out and cool completely on a wire rack.
≈ Trim the sides from each cake. Mix together the filling ingredients. Place the yellow cake on a chopping board and spread half of the filling on top. Place the pink cake on top and spread with the remaining filling. Top with the white cake. Dust with powdered sugar and slice to serve.

3 eggs
6 tbsp fine granulated sugar
¾ cup self rising flour
few drops of pink food coloring
few drops of yellow food coloring

For the filling
scant cup low-fat soft cheese, such as curd or cream cheese
2 tbsp powdered sugar

NUTRITION FACTS
Serving Size 1 (28g)

Calories 74	Calories from Fat 9
	% Daily Value
Total Fat 1g	2%
Saturated Fat 0g	2%
Monounsaturated Fat 0.5g	0%
Polyunsaturated Fat 0.2g	0%
Cholesterol 53mg	18%
Sodium 115mg	5%
Total Carbohydrate 13g	4%
Dietary Fiber 0g	1%
Sugars 7g	0%
Protein 2g	0%

Percent daily values are based on a 2000 calorie diet

GINGERBREAD

SERVES 16

Skim milk, prunes, and egg white are used in this classic cake to reduce the fat content. For an extra spicy flavor, add 1 teaspoon of ground allspice to the mixture as well as the ginger.

≈ Grease and line a 9-inch square pan. Sift the flour, salt, ground ginger, baking powder, and baking soda into a large bowl.
≈ Place the sugar, molasses, and syrup in a pan and heat gently to dissolve. Place the prunes in a food processor with 3 tablespoons of water and blend for 30 seconds until puréed. Add the milk to the sugar mixture and stir into the dry ingredients with the prunes, mixing well. Whisk the egg white until peaking, fold into the mixture and spoon into the prepared pan.

≈ Bake in the oven at 325°F for 55 minutes–1 hour or until firm. Cool in the pan for 10 minutes. Turn the cake out onto a wire rack and cool completely. Cut into 16 pieces. Dust with powdered sugar and top with chopped ginger.

4 cups all-purpose flour
dash of salt
1 tbsp ground ginger
1 tbsp baking powder
1 tsp baking soda
1 cup granulated brown sugar
½ cup molasses
½ cup corn syrup
⅔ cup dried pitted prunes
1¼ cups skim milk
1 egg white
powdered sugar for dusting
2 pieces stem ginger, chopped

NUTRITION FACTS
Serving Size 1 (107g)

Calories 267	Calories from Fat 0
	% Daily Value
Total Fat 0g	1%
Saturated Fat 0g	0%
Monounsaturated Fat 0.0g	0%
Polyunsaturated Fat 0.1g	0%
Cholesterol 0mg	0%
Sodium 231mg	10%
Total Carbohydrate 62g	21%
Dietary Fiber 2g	6%
Sugars 23g	0%
Protein 4g	0%

Percent daily values are based on a 2000 calorie diet

Gingerbread ▶

OAT AND ORANGE COOKIES

MAKES 20

These little cookies are hard to resist. Rolled in oatmeal, they have a crunchy outside, and softer inside which has a mild orange flavor.

3 tbsp polyunsaturated margarine

¼ cup granulated brown sugar

1 egg white, lightly beaten

2 tbsp skim milk

3 tbsp raisins

grated rind of 1 orange

1¼ cups self rising flour

⅓ cup oatmeal

strips of orange rind to decorate
   (optional)

≈ Cream the margarine and sugar together until light and fluffy. Add the egg white, milk, raisins, and orange rind. Fold in the flour and bring the mixture together to form a dough. Roll into 20 equal-sized balls.

≈ Place the oats in a shallow bowl, roll each dough ball in the oats to coat completely, pressing them on gently. Place the cookies on nonstick baking sheets, spacing well apart. Flatten each round slightly.

≈ Bake in the oven at 350°F for 15 minutes or until golden. Cool on a wire rack, decorate and store any leftovers in an airtight container.

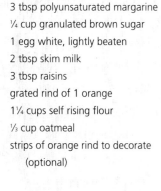

NUTRITION FACTS	
Serving Size 1 (20g)	
Calories 69	Calories from Fat 18
	% Daily Value
Total Fat 2g	3%
Saturated Fat 0g	2%
Monounsaturated Fat 0.8g	0%
Polyunsaturated Fat 0.6g	0%
Cholesterol 0mg	0%
Sodium 124mg	5%
Total Carbohydrate 12g	4%
Dietary Fiber 1g	2%
Sugars 4g	0%
Protein 1g	0%

Percent daily values are based on a 2000 calorie diet

RAISIN AND HONEY BREAD

SERVES 16

This loaf contains a high proportion of yogurt which gives it a white, light center.

≈ Mix the flour, baking powder, baking soda and salt in a large bowl. Whisk together the yogurt and egg whites and fold into the flour mixture with the raisins and honey.

≈ Grease a 2 lb loaf pan and spoon in the mixture. Bake in the oven at 425°F for 20 minutes until golden. Cool slightly and turn out of the pan. Serve warm.

2¼ cups all-purpose flour
1½ tsp baking powder
½ tsp baking soda
½ tsp salt
1¾ cups low-fat plain yogurt
2 egg whites
⅓ cup raisins
2 tbsp honey
polyunsaturated margarine for
    greasing

NUTRITION FACTS	
Serving Size 1 (53g)	
Calories 102	Calories from Fat 9
	% Daily Value
Total Fat 1g	1%
Saturated Fat 0g	2%
Monounsaturated Fat 0.2g	0%
Polyunsaturated Fat 0.1g	0%
Cholesterol 2mg	1%
Sodium 141mg	6%
Total Carbohydrate 20g	7%
Dietary Fiber 1g	2%
Sugars 6g	0%
Protein 4g	0%

Percent daily values are based on a 2000 calorie diet

CHOCOLATE BROWNIES

MAKES 16

Chocolate brownies in a low-fat book? They taste just as good as the real thing but have a slightly different texture. Keep in an airtight container if you can resist them for long enough.

≈ Grease and line a shallow 7-inch square cake pan.

≈ Place the prunes in a food processor with 3 tablespoons of water and blend to a purée. Transfer the purée to a mixing bowl and stir in the sugar, cocoa, flour, and baking powder. Whisk the egg whites until peaking and fold into the mixture. Pour into the prepared pan and level the surface.

≈ Bake in the oven at 350°F for 1 hour or until cooked through. Let the brownies cool in the pan for 10 minutes, then turn out onto a wire rack and cool completely. Cut into 16 squares, dust with powdered sugar and serve.

⅔ cup pitted dried prunes

¾ cup granulated brown sugar

3 tbsp unsweetened cocoa powder, sifted

½ cup all-purpose flour

1 tsp baking powder

3 egg whites

powdered sugar for dusting

NUTRITION FACTS

Serving Size 1 (36g)	
Calories 90	Calories from Fat 0

	% Daily Value
Total Fat 0g	0%
Saturated Fat 0g	0%
Monounsaturated Fat 0.0g	0%
Polyunsaturated Fat 0.0g	0%
Cholesterol 0mg	0%
Sodium 45mg	2%
Total Carbohydrate 22g	7%
Dietary Fiber 1g	3%
Sugars 17g	0%
Protein 1g	0%

Percent daily values are based on a 2000 calorie diet

SEED BREAD

SERVES 12

The seeds in this loaf add flavor and texture to the bread. Easy to eat, it is divided into six portions which are simply broken off for serving.

≈ Place the yeast, flour, sugar, and salt in a large bowl. Rub in the margarine and add half of each of the seeds. Stir in 1¼ cups tepid water and mix well. Bring the mixture together to form a soft dough. Knead the dough for 5 minutes on a lightly floured surface and break into six equal pieces.

≈ Lightly grease a deep 6 inch round cake pan. Shape each of the dough pieces into a round. Place five pieces around the edge of the pan and one in the center. Cover and let prove in a warm place for 1 hour or until doubled in size.

≈ Whisk the egg white and brush over the top of the dough. Sprinkle the remaining seeds onto the top of the dough, alternating the different types on each section of the loaf.

≈ Bake in the oven at 400°F for 30 minutes or until cooked through. The loaf should sound hollow when tapped on the base. Cool slightly and serve.

1 package active dry yeast

4 cups whole wheat flour

2 tsp fine granulated sugar

2 tsp salt

2 tbsp polyunsaturated margarine

2 tsp caraway seeds

2 tsp fennel seeds

2 tsp sesame seeds

1 egg white

NUTRITION FACTS

Serving Size 1 (48g)	
Calories 161	Calories from Fat 27

	% Daily Value
Total Fat 3g	5%
Saturated Fat 1g	3%
Monounsaturated Fat 1.0g	0%
Polyunsaturated Fat 0.9g	0%
Cholesterol 0mg	0%
Sodium 418mg	17%
Total Carbohydrate 30g	10%
Dietary Fiber 5g	21%
Sugars 1g	0%
Protein 6g	0%

Percent daily values are based on a 2000 calorie diet

Seed Bread ▶

HERBED CHEESE LOAF

SERVES 8

This loaf is best served warm straight from the oven to obtain the full flavor of the herbs and cheese.

1 package active dry yeast

1½ lb white bread flour

1 tsp salt

1 tsp fine granulated sugar

½ oz polyunsaturated margarine

3 tbsp fresh chopped parsley

¾ cup low-fat cheese, shredded

1 egg white

≈ Place the yeast, flour, salt, and sugar in a large mixing bowl. Rub in the margarine. Add the herbs and cheese and stir in 2 cups tepid water. Bring together to form a soft dough. Knead the dough on a lightly floured surface for 5–7 minutes until smooth.

≈ Divide the mixture into three equal portions. Roll each into a 14-inch sausage shape. Place the dough pieces side by side and cross over each other at the top, pressing together to seal. Continue working down the length of the dough, crossing alternate strands to form a braid. Seal the end by pressing together and fold both ends under the braid.

≈ Place the bread on a nonstick baking sheet, cover and leave in a warm place for 1 hour or until doubled in size.

≈ Lightly beat the egg white and brush over the loaf. Bake in the oven at 400°F for 30 minutes or until cooked through. The loaf will sound hollow when tapped on the base. Serve.

NUTRITION FACTS

Serving Size 1 (98g)

Calories 336   Calories from Fat 27

	% Daily Value
Total Fat 3g	5%
Saturated Fat 1g	3%
Monounsaturated Fat 0.8g	0%
Polyunsaturated Fat 1.0g	0%
Cholesterol 1mg	0%
Sodium 327mg	14%
Total Carbohydrate 63g	21%
Dietary Fiber 3g	10%
Sugars 1g	0%
Protein 12g	0%

Percent daily values are based on a 2000 calorie diet

WHOLE WHEAT SODA BREAD

SERVES 12

This yeast-free bread is based on an Irish recipe where it is traditionally served. Made with whole wheat flour for extra goodness, it is filling and ideal served with soups.

1½ cups all-purpose flour

1½ cups whole wheat flour

2 tsp baking soda

2 tsp cream of tartar

½ tsp salt

2 tbsp polyunsaturated margarine

1½ cups skim milk

2 egg whites

≈ Lightly grease and flour a baking sheet. Sift the flours, baking soda, cream of tartar, and salt into a bowl. Add the contents of the sieve to the bowl.

≈ Rub in the margarine and gradually mix in the milk and beaten egg whites to form a dough. Shape the mixture into a round on a lightly floured surface. Score into four triangles with a knife and place on the prepared baking sheet. Bake in the oven at 425°F for 30 minutes or until cooked. Serve warm.

NUTRITION FACTS

Serving Size 1 (71g)

Calories 139   Calories from Fat 18

	% Daily Value
Total Fat 2g	4%
Saturated Fat 0g	2%
Monounsaturated Fat 0.9g	0%
Polyunsaturated Fat 0.8g	0%
Cholesterol 1mg	0%
Sodium 355mg	15%
Total Carbohydrate 25g	8%
Dietary Fiber 2g	9%
Sugars 2g	0%
Protein 5g	0%

Percent daily values are based on a 2000 calorie diet

Whole Wheat Soda Bread ▶

PEAR UPSIDE-DOWN CAKE

SERVES 8

In this recipe, sliced pears are set on a caramel base and topped with a spicy sponge mixture. Once cooked, turn out and serve immediately with plain yogurt.

2 tbsp honey

2 tbsp granulated brown sugar

2 large pears, peeled, cored and sliced

4 tbsp polyunsaturated margarine

¼ cup fine granulated sugar

3 egg whites

1 cup self rising flour

2 tsp ground allspice

≈ Heat the honey and sugar in a pan until melted. Pour into a base lined 8-inch round cake pan. Arrange the pears around the base of the pan.

≈ Cream the margarine and sugar together until light and fluffy. Whisk the egg whites until peaking and fold into the mixture with the flour and allspice. Spoon on top of the pears.

≈ Bake in the oven at 350°F for 50 minutes or until risen and golden. Let sit for 5 minutes, then turn out onto a serving plate. Remove the lining paper and serve.

≈ Decorate with walnuts, but remember that nuts are high in fat and are best saved for special occasions.

NUTRITION FACTS	
Serving Size 1 (92g)	
Calories 190	Calories from Fat 54
	% Daily Value
Total Fat 6g	9%
Saturated Fat 1g	6%
Monounsaturated Fat 2.6g	0%
Polyunsaturated Fat 1.9g	0%
Cholesterol 0mg	0%
Sodium 287mg	12%
Total Carbohydrate 32g	11%
Dietary Fiber 2g	6%
Sugars 18g	0%
Protein 3g	0%

Percent daily values are based on a 2000 calorie diet

ROCKY MOUNTAIN BUNS

MAKES 12

There is a hint of coffee in these fun-to-eat small buns. The marshmallows and raisins give them a "rocky," uneven appearance.

2½ cups self rising flour

½ tsp salt

¼ cup polyunsaturated margarine

2 tbsp fine granulated sugar

3 tbsp golden raisins

1 oz mini marshmallows

⅔ cup skim milk

1 tbsp coffee extract

powdered sugar for dusting

≈ Sieve the flour and salt into a bowl. Rub in the margarine until the mixture resembles bread crumbs. Stir in the sugar, raisins, and marshmallows.

≈ Mix together the milk and coffee extract and stir into the mixture to form a soft dough. Place 12 equal-sized spoonfuls of mixture on a nonstick baking sheet, spacing slightly apart.

≈ Bake in the oven at 425°F for 20 minutes until risen and golden. Cool on a wire rack and serve.

NUTRITION FACTS	
Serving Size 1 (58g)	
Calories 172	Calories from Fat 36
	% Daily Value
Total Fat 4g	6%
Saturated Fat 1g	4%
Monounsaturated Fat 1.7g	0%
Polyunsaturated Fat 1.3g	0%
Cholesterol 0mg	0%
Sodium 481mg	20%
Total Carbohydrate 30g	10%
Dietary Fiber 1g	4%
Sugars 10g	0%
Protein 3g	0%

Percent daily values are based on a 2000 calorie diet

Pear Upside-down Cake ▶

1⅓ cups dried apricots, chopped

4 tbsp unsweetened orange juice

6 tbsp polyunsaturated margarine,
melted

4 tbsp honey

½ cup semolina flour

1 cup plus 2 tbsp all-purpose flour

NUTRITION FACTS	
Serving Size 1 (95g)	
Calories 223	Calories from Fat 54
	% Daily Value
Total Fat 6g	9%
Saturated Fat 1g	6%
Monounsaturated Fat 2.6g	0%
Polyunsaturated Fat 1.9g	0%
Cholesterol 0mg	0%
Sodium 69mg	3%
Total Carbohydrate 40g	13%
Dietary Fiber 2g	9%
Sugars 17g	0%
Protein 4g	0%

Percent daily values are based on a 2000 calorie diet

APRICOT BARS

MAKES 8

These are very filling, healthy fruit bars. A delicious apricot purée is sandwiched between a shortcake mixture.

≈ Lightly grease a 7-inch square cake pan. Place the apricots in a pan with the orange juice and simmer for 5 minutes. Drain if the juice has not been absorbed by the fruit.

≈ Heat the margarine and honey in a pan until melted. Add the semolina and flour and mix well. Press half of the semolina mixture into the base of the prepared pan. Spoon on the fruit mixture and top with the remaining semolina mix, covering the fruit completely.

≈ Bake in the oven at 375°F for 35 minutes until golden. Cool for 5 minutes in the pan, then cut into eight bars. Remove from the pan and cool completely.

¼ cup polyunsaturated margarine

1¼ cups granulated brown sugar

2 egg whites

1¼ cups all-purpose flour

3 tbsp unsweetened cocoa powder,
sifted

¼ tsp baking soda

¼ tsp baking powder

1 cup skim milk

powdered sugar and cocoa for
dusting

NUTRITION FACTS	
Serving Size 1 (75g)	
Calories 195	Calories from Fat 36
	% Daily Value
Total Fat 4g	6%
Saturated Fat 1g	4%
Monounsaturated Fat 1.7g	0%
Polyunsaturated Fat 1.2g	0%
Cholesterol 0mg	0%
Sodium 102mg	4%
Total Carbohydrate 38g	13%
Dietary Fiber 0g	1%
Sugars 26g	0%
Protein 3g	0%

Percent daily values are based on a 2000 calorie diet

LOW-FAT CHOCOLATE CAKE

SERVES 12

This chocolate cake is very rich and a small slice will satisfy any chocoholic for a while.

≈ Grease and flour an 8-inch round cake pan. Cream the margarine and sugar in a bowl until light and fluffy. Add the egg whites and whisk into the mixture until thick.

≈ Place the flour, cocoa, baking soda, and baking powder in a separate bowl. Add the milk gradually to the egg white mixture, alternating with the dry ingredients. Pour the mixture into the prepared pan.

≈ Bake in the oven at 350°F for 1 hour or until cooked through. Let cool completely in the pan. Turn out and dust with the powdered sugar and cocoa. Serve.

Apricot Bars ▶

CARROT AND PRUNE CAKE

SERVES 12

This recipe is traditionally high in fat, but this version uses prunes in its place and only uses the whites of the eggs. Take extra care folding in the egg whites as a heavy hand will result in a heavy cake.

8 oz carrots

15 oz can prunes in fruit juice

1¼ cups granulated brown sugar

2½ cups self rising flour

grated rind of 1 orange

3 tbsp semolina flour

3 egg whites

For the icing

¾ cup low-fat soft cheese

1 tbsp powdered sugar, sieved

ground cinnamon and orange rind
    to decorate

NUTRITION FACTS

Serving Size 1 (114g)	
Calories 228	Calories from Fat 0

	% Daily Value
Total Fat 0g	1%
Saturated Fat 0g	0%
Monounsaturated Fat 0.0g	0%
Polyunsaturated Fat 0.1g	0%
Cholesterol 0mg	0%
Sodium 360mg	15%
Total Carbohydrate 53g	18%
Dietary Fiber 2g	8%
Sugars 28g	0%
Protein 4g	0%

Percent daily values are based on a 2000 calorie diet

≈ Grease and base line an 8-inch deep cake pan. Shred the carrots and place in a bowl. Drain the prunes and discard the juice and pits. Blend the prunes in a food processor for 30 seconds and add to the carrot with the sugar.

≈ Add the flour, orange rind, and semolina to the mixture, stirring well. Whisk the egg whites until peaks form and fold into the mixture. Spoon into the prepared pan and level the surface.

≈ Bake in the oven at 375°F for 45 minutes or until cooked through. Cool in the pan for 10 minutes, turn out and cool completely on a wire rack.

≈ Mix together the cream cheese and powdered sugar for the icing. Spread on top of the cake. Decorate and serve.

126

INDEX

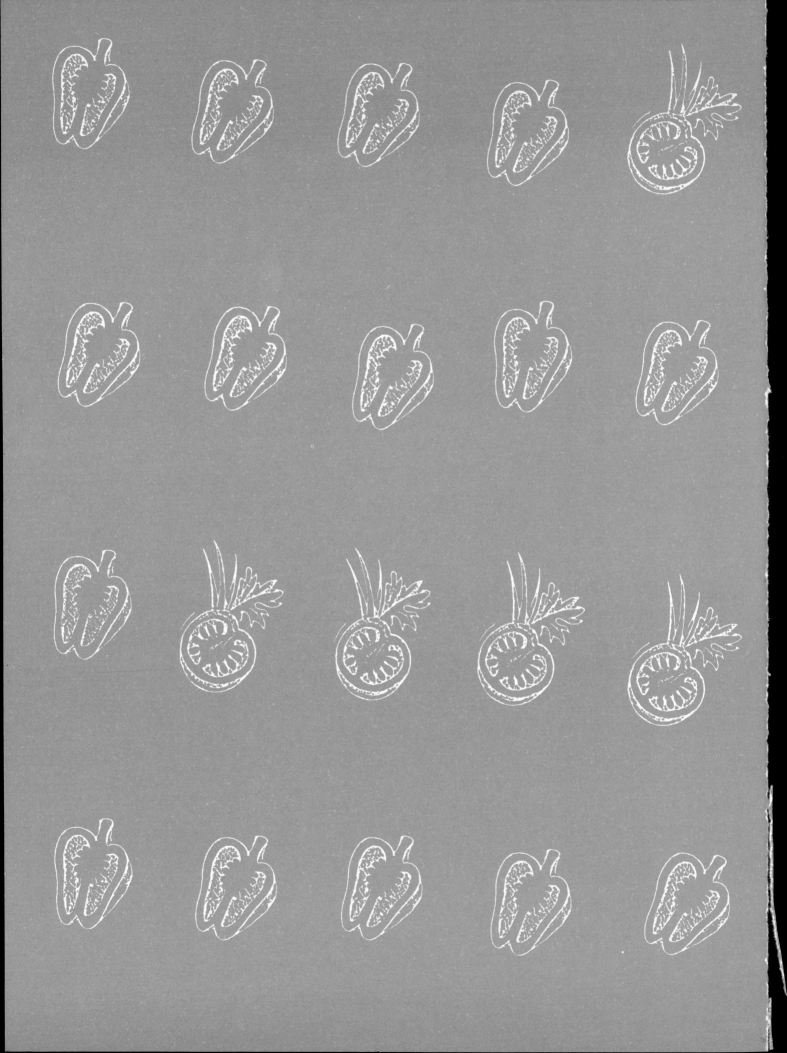